# collections

# Close Reader

**GRADE 6**

**Program Consultants:**
Kylene Beers
Martha Hougen
Carol Jago
William L. McBride
Erik Palmer
Lydia Stack

**Cover, Title Page Photo Credits:** ©AStock/Corbis

Printed in the U.S.A.

ISBN 978-0-544-08760-6

2 3 4 5 6 7 8 9 10 1421 22 21 20 19 18 17 16 15 14 13

4500432161 A B C D E F G

## COLLECTION 1
# Facing Fear


**SHORT STORY**
*from* The Jumping Tree — René Saldaña, Jr. — 3

**MAGAZINE ARTICLE**
Face Your Fears: Choking Under Pressure Is Every Athlete's Worst Nightmare — Dana Hudepohl — 9

**MAGAZINE ARTICLE**
Face Your Fears and Scare the Phobias Out of Your Brain — Jason Koebler — 13

## COLLECTION 2
# Animal Intelligence


**SHORT STORY**
The Pod — Maureen Crane Wartski — 19

**INFORMATIONAL TEXT**
Can Animals Feel and Think? — DeShawn Jones — 25

**SCIENCE WRITING**
Bats! — Mary Kay Carson — 29

**Visit hmhfyi.com** for current articles and informational texts.

COLLECTION **3**

# Dealing with Disaster

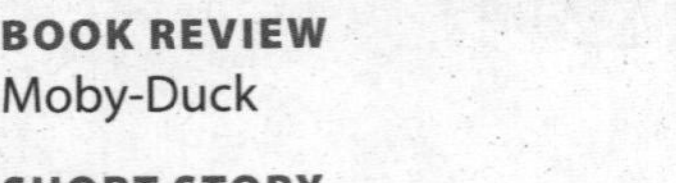


| | | |
|---|---|---|
| **BOOK REVIEW** | | |
| Moby-Duck | David Holahan | 37 |
| **SHORT STORY** | | |
| There Will Come Soft Rains | Ray Bradbury | 43 |
| **NEWSPAPER ARTICLE** | | |
| On the Titanic, Defined by What They Wore | Guy Trebay | 53 |

COLLECTION **4**

# Making Your Voice Heard


| | | |
|---|---|---|
| **INFORMATIONAL TEXTS** | | |
| Views on Zoos | | 63 |
| Functions of a Zoo | | 63 |
| Sonia's Blog: Who I Am, What I Do—Every Day | | 64 |
| Association of Zoos and Aquariums | | 66 |
| Innocent and Imprisoned | Robert McGuinness | 67 |
| **SHORT STORY** | | |
| What Do Fish Have to Do with Anything? | Avi | 69 |

COLLECTION **5**

# Decisions That Matter


**BIOGRAPHY**
Community Hero: Chief Wilma Mankiller — Susannah Abbey — 87

**AUTOBIOGRAPHY**
*from* Every Day Is a New Day — Wilma Mankiller — 91

**POEM**
The Light—Ah! The Light — Joyce Sidman — 97


COLLECTION **6**

# What Tales Tell


**GREEK MYTH**
Medusa's Head — *retold by* Olivia E. Coolidge — 101

**POEM**
Medusa — Agha Shahid Ali — 113

**Comparing Versions** — 115

**NOVEL**
Tom's Meeting with the Prince. *from* The Prince and the Pauper — Mark Twain — 115

**DRAMA**
*from* The Prince and the Pauper — Mark Twain, *dramatized by* Joellen Bland — 121

**GRAPHIC STORY**
*from* The Prince and the Pauper — Marvel Comics — 125




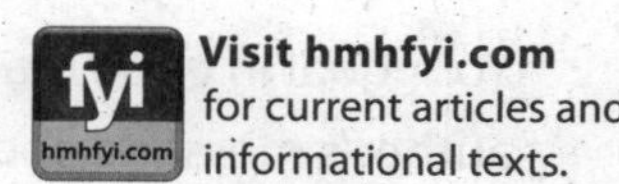

**Visit hmhfyi.com** for current articles and informational texts.

# Becoming A Close Reader

## READING THE TEXTS

Challenging literary and informational texts require close reading to understand and appreciate their meanings fully. These texts may have difficult language or complex structures that become clear only with careful study. To fully understand these demanding texts, you need to learn how to read and reread slowly and deliberately.

The Close Reader provides many opportunities to practice close reading. To become a close reader,

- read each text in the Close Reader slowly all the way through.
- take time to think about and respond to the READ and REREAD prompts that help focus your reading.
- cite specific textual evidence to support your analysis of the selection.

Your goal in close reading is to build useful knowledge as you analyze the author's message and appreciate the author's craft.

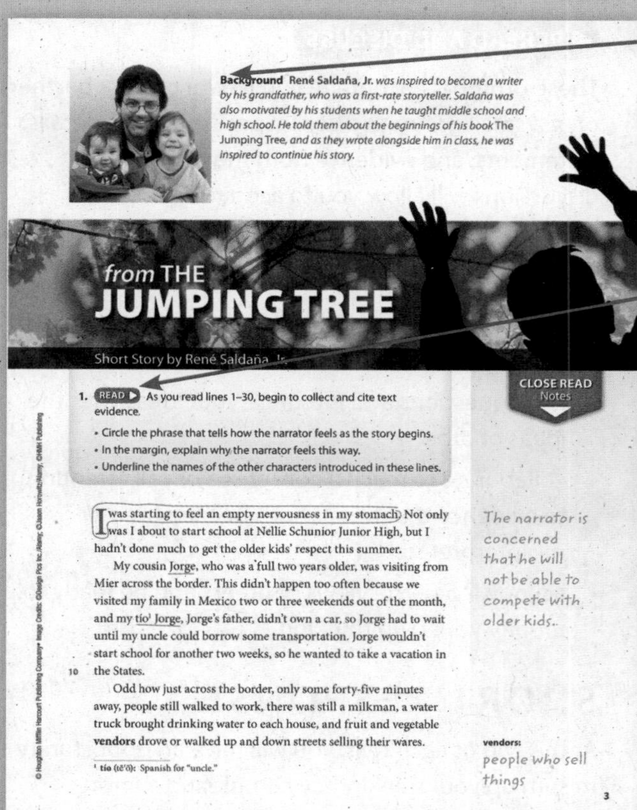

**Background** René Saldaña, Jr. *was inspired to become a writer by his grandfather, who was a first-rate storyteller. Saldaña was also motivated by his students when he taught middle school and high school. He told them about the beginnings of his book* The Jumping Tree, *and as they wrote alongside him in class, he was inspired to continue his story.*

# *from* THE JUMPING TREE

Short Story by René Saldaña, Jr.

CLOSE READ Notes

1. READ ▶ As you read lines 1–30, begin to collect and cite text evidence.
   - Circle the phrase that tells how the narrator feels as the story begins.
   - In the margin, explain why the narrator feels this way.
   - Underline the names of the other characters introduced in these lines.

I was starting to feel an empty nervousness in my stomach. Not only was I about to start school at Nellie Schunior Junior High, but I hadn't done much to get the older kids' respect this summer.

My cousin Jorge, who was a full two years older, was visiting from Mier across the border. This didn't happen too often because we visited my family in Mexico two or three weekends out of the month, and my tío[1] Jorge, Jorge's father, didn't own a car, so Jorge had to wait until my uncle could borrow some transportation. Jorge wouldn't start school for another two weeks, so he wanted to take a vacation in the States.

Odd how just across the border, only some forty-five minutes away, people still walked to work, there was still a milkman, a water truck brought drinking water to each house, and fruit and vegetable **vendors** drove or walked up and down streets selling their wares.

*The narrator is concerned that he will not be able to compete with older kids.*

**vendors:** *people who sell things*

[1] **tío** (tē'ō): Spanish for "uncle."

3

## Background

This paragraph provides information about the text you are about to read. It helps you understand the context of the selection through additional information about the author, the subject, or the time period in which the text was written.

## READ ▶

With practice, you can learn how to be a close reader. Questions and specific instructions at the beginning of the selection and on the bottom of the pages will guide your close reading of each text.

These questions and instructions

- refer to specific sections of the text.
- ask you to look for and mark up specific information in the text.
- prompt you to record inferences and text analysis in the side margins.
- help you begin to collect and cite text evidence.

CLOSE READ Notes

When I'd visit my cousin, he'd always make certain I had a good time. We'd spend hours on end in his father's carpentry shop sawing blocks of wood into rough imitations of cars and planes. We'd shave planks of wood until they felt smooth on the palms of our hands or our cheeks. We'd use the shavings later on for **kindling** or confetti, and we'd dig our fingers into the mountains of sawdust, sometimes as deep as our elbows.

**kindling:**

So, when he came up to Peñitas, I wanted to make sure there was always something doing. Since he was older, I didn't want to do things that were for kids, but I didn't know exactly how to entertain him.

At the beginning of summer, Tío Nardo had hammered a few slats of wood to my granddad's mesquite tree in the middle of the backyard, called it a tree house, and we were set. It was just like in *The Brady Bunch.*[2] Only their tree house actually resembled a house, with its walls, windows, roof, and floor. We had to imagine all that. All we had, really, were flat places to sit on. But it was enough for us.

One day after Jorge arrived, Ricky was over, and we came up with a jumping and gymnastics competition. Actually, Ricky came up with the idea because he was good at that stuff. He was always saying,

[2] **The Brady Bunch:** popular TV show of the 1960s and '70s.

2. ◀ REREAD Reread lines 15–24. What can you infer about the narrator's feelings toward his cousin? Underline text evidence that supports your inference.

3. READ ▶ As you read lines 31–70, continue to cite textual evidence.
   - Underline text that reveals the narrator's thoughts and feelings about jumping.
   - Circle details that describe the setting.
   - In the margin, explain the narrator's thoughts as his turn to jump approaches.

4



## Vocabulary

Critical vocabulary words appear in the margin throughout most selections. Consult a print or online dictionary to define the word on your own.

When you see a vocabulary word in the margin,

- write the definition of each word in the margin.
- be sure your definition fits the context of the word as it is used in the text.
- check your definition by substituting it in place of the vocabulary word from the text. Your definition should make sense in the context of the selection.

## ◀ REREAD

To further guide your close reading, REREAD questions at the bottom of the page will

- ask you to focus on a close analysis of a smaller chunk of text.
- prompt you to analyze literary elements and devices, as well as the meaning and structure of informational text.
- help you go back into the text and "read between the lines" to uncover meanings and central ideas.

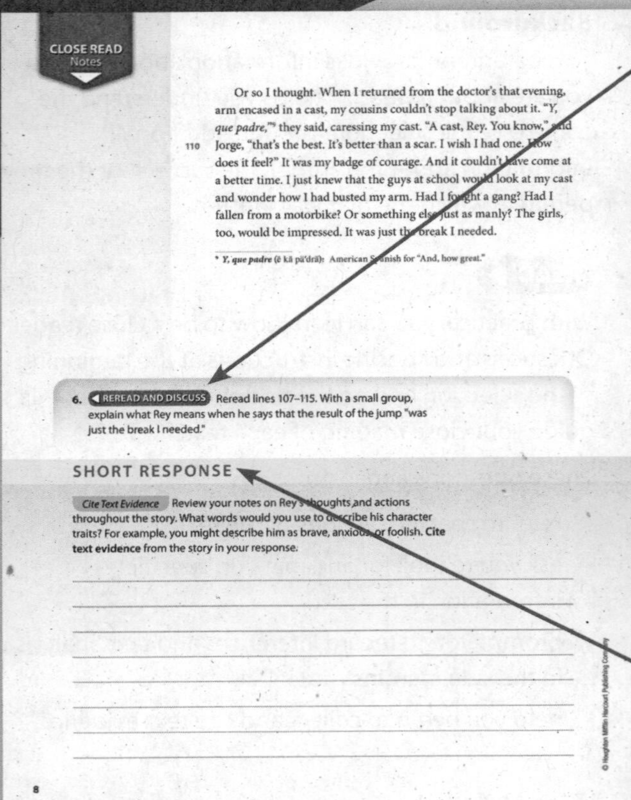

CLOSE READ Notes

Or so I thought. When I returned from the doctor's that evening, arm encased in a cast, my cousins couldn't stop talking about it. "*Y, que padre,*"* they said, caressing my cast. "A cast, Rey. You know," said Jorge, "that's the best. It's better than a scar. I wish I had one. How does it feel?" It was my badge of courage. And it couldn't have come at a better time. I just knew that the guys at school would look at my cast and wonder how I had busted my arm. Had I fought a gang? Had I fallen from a motorbike? Or something else just as manly? The girls, too, would be impressed. It was just the break I needed.

* ***Y, que padre*** (ē kä pä′drā): American Spanish for "And, how great."

6. REREAD AND DISCUSS Reread lines 107–115. With a small group, explain what Rey means when he says that the result of the jump "was just the break I needed."

SHORT RESPONSE

*Cite Text Evidence* Review your notes on Rey's thoughts and actions throughout the story. What words would you use to describe his character traits? For example, you might describe him as brave, anxious, or foolish. **Cite text evidence** from the story in your response.

8



## ◀ REREAD AND DISCUSS

These prompts encourage you to work with a partner or in a small group to discuss specific events, details, statements, and evidence from the text. These discussions will allow you to acquire and share knowledge about the texts you are reading.

As you engage in these discussions,

- be sure to cite specific text evidence in support of your statements.
- pose questions and integrate your ideas with the ideas of others.
- collaborate to reach a consensus or call attention to evidence that might have been missed or misinterpreted.
- acknowledge the views of others and be ready to modify your own thinking.

## SHORT RESPONSE

At the end of each text, you will have an opportunity to sum up your thinking by completing a Short Response. The Short Response represents a place to convey some of the ideas you have developed through close reading of the text.

When you write your Short Response,

- review all of your margin notes and REREAD answers.
- circle or highlight evidence from your notes that supports your position or point of view.
- clearly state your point of view and support it with reasons.
- cite specific text evidence to support your reasons.

COLLECTION 1

# Facing Fear

COLLECTION 1

# Facing Fear

"Do one thing every day that scares you."

—Eleanor Roosevelt


SHORT STORY

*from* The Jumping Tree — **René Saldaña, Jr.**

MAGAZINE ARTICLE

Face Your Fears: Choking Under Pressure Is Every Athlete's Worst Nightmare — **Dana Hudepohl**

MAGAZINE ARTICLE

Face Your Fears and Scare the Phobias Out of Your Brain — **Jason Koebler**

**Background** René Saldaña, Jr. *was inspired to become a writer by his grandfather, who was a first-rate storyteller. Saldaña was also motivated by his students when he taught middle school and high school. He told them about the beginnings of his book* The Jumping Tree, *and as they wrote alongside him in class, he was inspired to continue his story.*

# *from* THE JUMPING TREE

Short Story by René Saldaña, Jr.

1. **READ ▶** As you read lines 1–30, begin to collect and cite text evidence.
   - Circle the phrase that tells how the narrator feels as the story begins.
   - In the margin, explain why the narrator feels this way.
   - Underline the names of the other characters introduced in these lines.

I was starting to feel an empty nervousness in my stomach. Not only was I about to start school at Nellie Schunior Junior High, but I hadn't done much to get the older kids' respect this summer.

The narrator is concerned that he will not be able to compete with older kids.

My cousin Jorge, who was a full two years older, was visiting from Mier across the border. This didn't happen too often because we visited my family in Mexico two or three weekends out of the month, and my tío[1] Jorge, Jorge's father, didn't own a car, so Jorge had to wait until my uncle could borrow some transportation. Jorge wouldn't start school for another two weeks, so he wanted to take a vacation in the States.

Odd how just across the border, only some forty-five minutes away, people still walked to work, there was still a milkman, a water truck brought drinking water to each house, and fruit and vegetable **vendors** drove or walked up and down streets selling their wares.

**vendors:** people who sell things

[1] **tío** (tē′ō): Spanish for "uncle."

When I'd visit my cousin, he'd always make certain I had a good time. We'd spend hours on end in his father's carpentry shop sawing blocks of wood into rough imitations of cars and planes. We'd shave planks of wood until they felt smooth on the palms of our hands or our cheeks. We'd use the shavings later on for **kindling** or confetti, and we'd dig our fingers into the mountains of sawdust, sometimes as deep as our elbows.

**kindling:**

So, when he came up to Peñitas, I wanted to make sure there was always something doing. Since he was older, I didn't want to do things that were for kids, but I didn't know exactly how to entertain him.

At the beginning of summer, Tío Nardo had hammered a few slats of wood to my granddad's mesquite tree in the middle of the backyard, called it a tree house, and we were set. It was just like in *The Brady Bunch*.[2] Only their tree house actually resembled a house, with its walls, windows, roof, and floor. We had to imagine all that. All we had, really, were flat places to sit on. But it was enough for us.

One day after Jorge arrived, Ricky was over, and we came up with a jumping and gymnastics competition. Actually, Ricky came up with the idea because he was good at that stuff. He was always saying,

2 **The Brady Bunch:** popular TV show of the 1960s and '70s.

**2.** **◀ REREAD** Reread lines 15–24. What can you infer about the narrator's feelings toward his cousin? Underline text evidence that supports your inference.

**3.** **READ ▶** As you read lines 31–70, continue to cite textual evidence.

- Underline text that reveals the narrator's thoughts and feelings about jumping.
- Circle details that describe the setting.
- In the margin, explain the narrator's thoughts as his turn to jump approaches.

*"I had to go through with this deal. I had to prove that I could belong. . . ."*

"Look at this," and he'd tumble, pop a cartwheel, flip backward, or walk on his hands. Once he even walked across the top of a fence like a tightrope walker. Its sharp points didn't seem to bother him.

Ricky explained the rules as we stood under the **mammoth** mesquite: "Okay, we're going to climb the tree and start from there." He pointed to the slat where I normally sat. "Then jump down to that branch there and grab hold." His finger slid across the sky from the plank to a branch that stretched out below it. Easy enough. "Then whoever can do the best trick is the winner and king of the world."

**mammoth:**

"What do you mean by trick?" asked Jorge.

"You know, flips, swinging back and forth, then letting go, seeing who can land the fanciest."

All this time I'm thinking, *Okay, jump, grab, let go, and pray I land standing. No fancy-schmancy stuff for me. Just do the thing.*

But Jorge was the oldest of us, and the strongest; Ricky was the gymnast; and I was the youngest and the smallest, the one who had something to prove to these guys. I had to go through with this deal. I had to prove that I could belong to this group, could be a man.

"*Orale pues,*"[3] said Jorge. "Let's climb up."

And so we did, hand over hand, foot after foot, until we all reached the top and we **sidled** to the edge of the jumping place. When I saw how far the branch was from this spot, then how far the ground was from that branch, I decided to do the minimum, a jump and release. After all, I was only in the summer after my fifth-grade year. What could they expect?

**sidle:**

[3] ***orale pues*** (o·ra′lā pwäs): Spanish slang meaning "let's go, then" or "all right, then."

CLOSE READ Notes

Jorge went first. Ricky and I stood back, watching. My Mexican jumping bean heart was making it hard to concentrate on the task at hand. Even at this age I knew that people could learn a lot from their bodies' reactions to a situation: hand over open fire burns: remove hand immediately; hunger pangs: eat; heart grasping at sides of throat fighting to get out alongside that morning's breakfast: don't jump!

But, I am Mexican. I could not—strike that—would not back down. I would do the deed. It was a question of manhood. *¿Macho o mujeringa? ¡Pues macho!*[4]

Jorge screamed "*¡Aiee!*" and jumped. He swung like a trapeze artist at the Circus Vargas.[5] I whistled. Then I was one step closer to having to jump.

Ricky stepped up. "We'll see you down there, *primo*,"[6] he said.

"Yeah—down there." I forced a smile.

He jumped and it was like he and the branch were one. The rough bark of the mesquite melted into a smooth bar in his hands. He

[4] ***¿Macho o mujeringa? ¡Pues macho!*** (mä'cho ō moo'hār-ē'ä): Spanish slang for "Manly or weak and cowardly? Manly!"

[5] **Circus Vargas:** California-based traveling circus.

[6] ***primo*** (prē'mō): Spanish for "cousin," literally, but also used to mean "pal" or "close friend."

**4.** **REREAD** Reread lines 48–67. Why does the narrator decide to go through with the jump? Make an inference about the narrator based on his reasoning. Support your answer with explicit textual evidence.

**5.** **READ** As you read lines 71–115, continue to cite textual evidence.

- Underline details that convey the narrator's fear as he jumps.
- Circle details that suggest the narrator has a sense of humor about the events.



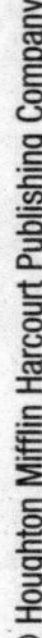

swung forward, let go, twisted, caught the bar again, swung toward me, flipped, all the while holding on to the branch, released, flipped in the air once, and stuck the landing. A perfect 10, even from the Russian judge.

I was next.

"*Orale*,[7] jump!" It sounded like an echo, they were so far away. I glanced down at them. A big mistake. My stomach was a better jumper than I because it was already flipping and turning. But I was at the edge of the board. I'd made a **contract** with myself, for my sake, signed in blood.

**contract:**

I began to rock back and forth, back and forth, back and forth, trying for courage.

The time had come. It was my destiny to fly, to live on the very edge of life, a life James Bond would be jealous of. So I dug my toes into my tennis shoes, took a deep breath, fought closing my eyes, stretched out my arms and did it.

I saw myself from below somehow. My body like Superman's flying over Metropolis. The branch growing bigger, closer. Within reach. All I had to do was to grab hold now. Just let the momentum[8] carry me toward the branch. The bark, rough on my palms, would be my safe place. All I had to do was close my fingers around the branch. Then swing and . . .

But my chubby little soon-to-be-sixth-grade fingers failed me.

I felt the branch slipping from my fingers. And so, like Superman confronted by kryptonite, I fell.

As the ground came closer, I tried to remember my PE coach's exact advice on how to fall. Had he told his little bunch of munchkins to roll onto our backs, or to put out our arms and hands? I had only a split second to make up my mind.

I stretched out my arms to break my fall.

What broke was my left wrist. When I rolled over and looked at the sky, I knew I had failed.

[7] ***orale:*** Spanish slang meaning "let's do it" or "let's go."

[8] **momentum:** the characteristic of a moving body that is caused by its mass and its motion.

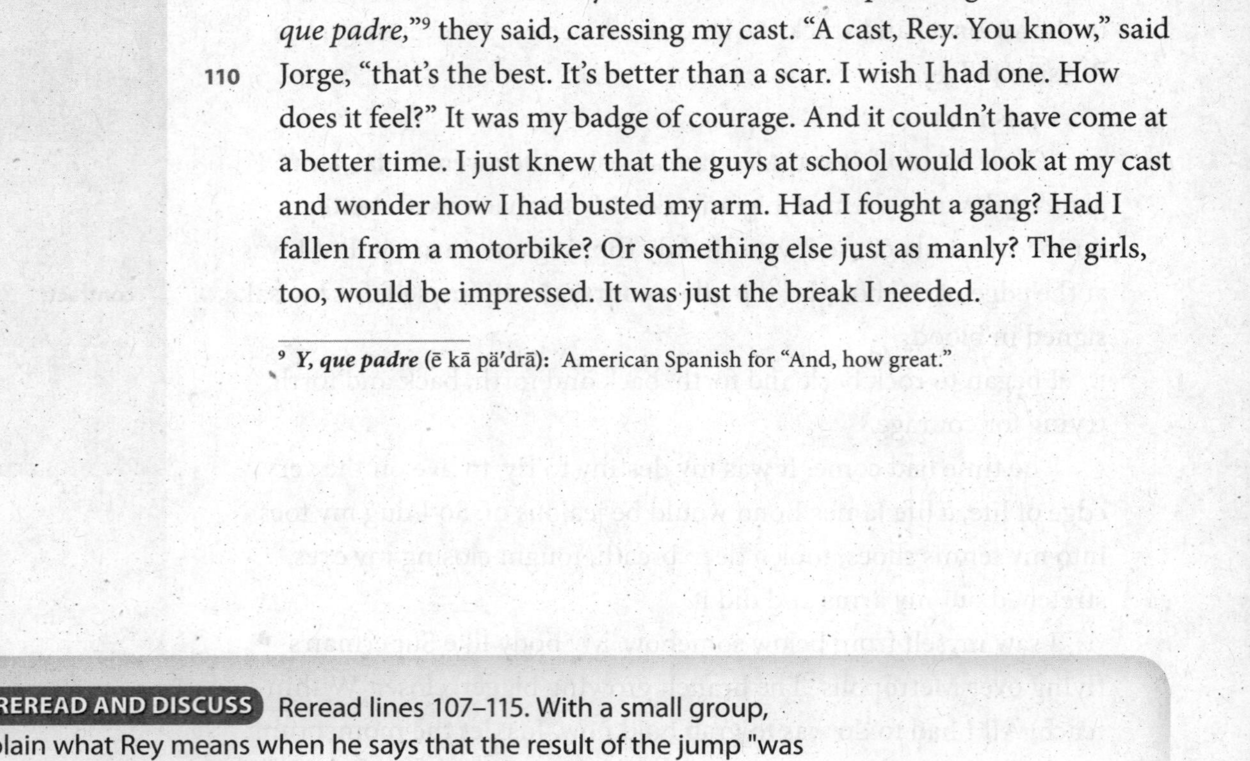

Or so I thought. When I returned from the doctor's that evening, arm encased in a cast, my cousins couldn't stop talking about it. "*Y, que padre,*"[9] they said, caressing my cast. "A cast, Rey. You know," said Jorge, "that's the best. It's better than a scar. I wish I had one. How does it feel?" It was my badge of courage. And it couldn't have come at a better time. I just knew that the guys at school would look at my cast and wonder how I had busted my arm. Had I fought a gang? Had I fallen from a motorbike? Or something else just as manly? The girls, too, would be impressed. It was just the break I needed.

[9] ***Y, que padre*** (ē kā pä'drā): American Spanish for "And, how great."

6. **REREAD AND DISCUSS** Reread lines 107–115. With a small group, explain what Rey means when he says that the result of the jump "was just the break I needed."

## SHORT RESPONSE

*Cite Text Evidence* Review your notes on Rey's thoughts and actions throughout the story. What words would you use to describe his character traits? For example, you might describe him as brave, anxious, or foolish. **Cite text evidence** from the story in your response.

**Background** *In athletics,* choking *refers to the failure to perform well during a key moment. For example, a golfer who misses an easy putt in the closing moments of a tournament is said to have "choked." In this article from* Sports Illustrated for Women, *three competitors offer their advice on how to handle fear and stress effectively while dealing with pressure to succeed.*

# Face Your Fears:
## Choking Under Pressure Is Every Athlete's Worst Nightmare

Magazine Article by Dana Hudepohl

CLOSE READ Notes

1. READ ▶ As you read lines 1–31, begin to collect and cite text evidence.
   - In the margin, briefly explain what is happening in lines 1–7.
   - Circle the key to Wilkinson's victory and the reaction of the fans (lines 8–12).
   - Underline details that describe Wilkinson's experience at her first international meet.

As she stood on the 10-meter platform at the Sydney Olympics, Laura Wilkinson knew she had to nail her fourth dive to clinch the gold. The pressure was intense: Head-to-head against the toughest divers in the world, she had to be flawless. "In a way I felt I was putting more pressure on myself than I could handle," says Wilkinson, 23. "But I felt like I had nothing to lose. There are more important things than fear."

With that calm attitude, she aced her fourth and fifth dives and won the gold. Her upset victory (she went from fifth to first after three dives) stunned competitors and fans. The key to Wilkinson's victory? Confidence, which was something she had worked on developing in her training.

"When you push away your nerves and refuse to think about them, they come on full force at the most important time: right during the meet," says Wilkinson. So, alone in her hotel room in Sydney, Wilkinson faced her fears the night before the final round of diving. "I let everything hit me: What would happen if I did well? What would happen if I did badly? What am I afraid of?" she recalls. "I was literally shaking just thinking about it, feeling scared and nervous. When I had the courage to stand up to what I was feeling, it didn't seem so bad anymore. I was able to move on."

Wilkinson knows what it's like to get hung up in doubts and anxieties. At her first international meet, she says she was seized by a feeling of near panic. "I was afraid of embarrassing myself and [as a result] I just choked," she says. It took her several meets to get over the experience, which sports psychologists say is not unusual.

"Every player chokes at some point—it's a natural response to competitive stress," says Todd Ryska, a professor of sport psychology at the University of Texas-San Antonio. "Athletes fear it most because of the stigma. No one wants to be the one everyone's talking about in the locker room."

## Find Your Focus

Choking is not a mistake out of nowhere like a shanked[1] golf shot; it's usually the result of misplaced focus. Athletes who avoid choking concentrate on the process (what do I have to do right now?), which is

[1] **shank:** a golf term meaning "to accidentally hit a golf ball with the wrong part of the golf club."

**2.** **REREAD** Reread lines 13–21. Wilkinson says confidence was the key to her Olympic victory. In the margin, list two details that support her statement.

**3.** **READ** As you read lines 32–51, underline the negative effects of fear and stress on Barb Lindquist at her first big meet.

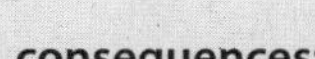

a positive mental approach. Those who choke tend to dwell on the outcome (what will happen if I don't win?) and its potentially unpleasant **consequences.**

consequences:

Letting your attention wander can also lead to trouble. Barb Lindquist, who swam for Stanford from 1987 to 1991, recalls how she felt at her first big meet (the U.S. Open) as she listened to the announcer reciting the accomplishments of her competitors. "I was 16 and I was next to a swimmer that I had read about. I got really flustered by hearing her accomplishments," she says. "I didn't concentrate on my race and was all shaky afterward. I finished last."

Now 31 and a triathlete,[2] Lindquist hasn't had any problems since then. While swimming, she repeats to herself the words "long and strong." On the bike she thinks about her pedal **technique**, and while running she visualizes balloons pulling up her legs to make her feel light. "If you're thinking about each of those things along the way and pushing yourself, you can't really choke," says Lindquist, who finished 2000 ranked seventh in the world.

technique:

Once choking symptoms kick in they're difficult to stop. Libbie Hickman, 35, found this out when she was running the 5,000 meters at the '96 Olympic trials. Hickman led until the last 100 meters, when three runners passed her. "I remember thinking, I'm not doing it. I'm not going to make the team," she says. "As soon as you start focusing on the negative you're dead."

[2] **triathlete:** a person who participates in a three-part athletic contest, which generally includes swimming, biking, and running.

4. **◀ REREAD AND DISCUSS** With a small group, discuss the main ideas the writer presents under the heading "Find Your Focus." Include facts and examples in lines 32–37 and the specific experiences of Barb Lindquist in your discussion.

5. **READ ▶** Read lines 52–68. In the margin, summarize Hickman's experiences at the 1996 and 2000 Olympic trials.

What Hickman learned from that experience helped her at the 2000 trials. "I started getting passed in the last lap, and the fear of coming in fourth again jumped in my head," she says. "But instead of letting that fear sit there, I threw it out, focused on the job that needed to be done and saw the finish line." The result: She finished third.

## It's Just a Game

**perspective:**

If you have a bad experience, keep it in **perspective.** "Not to minimize the importance of competition, but it's still only a portion of life," says Ryska. Your friends and teammates will still accept you even when you don't perform up to expectations—theirs or yours.

"You have to look forward," says Lindquist. "You only fail in a race if you haven't learned something from it."

**6.** **REREAD** Reread lines 63–68. Summarize the important idea under the heading "It's Just a Game."

## SHORT RESPONSE

*Cite Text Evidence* What is the central idea of this article? Review your reading notes, and **cite text evidence** that supports this idea.

**Background** *It is wise to be afraid of things that can hurt you. But when a fear is excessive and not based on reality, it becomes a phobia. In his article for* U.S. News & World Report, *science journalist* **Jason Koebler** *examines how a new form of therapy may be the first step to completely eliminating fears and phobias from our brains in the near future.*

# Face Your Fears and Scare the Phobias Out of Your Brain

Magazine Article by Jason Koebler

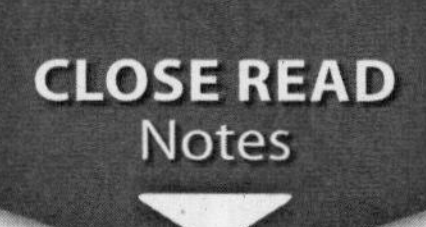


1. READ ▶ As you read lines 1–22, begin to collect and cite text evidence.
   - In the margin, restate the main idea in lines 1–4.
   - Underline text that explains why a person may choose to undergo "exposure therapy."
   - In the margin, list the steps that participants follow (lines 18–22).

It turns out facing your fears really does work—researchers at Northwestern University have found that just one positive **exposure** to spiders had lasting effects in people with arachnophobia[1] six months later.

**exposure:**

The parts of the brain responsible for producing fear remained relatively inactive six months after patients underwent a single two-hour "exposure therapy" session in which they were able to touch a live tarantula. The brain changes were seen immediately after therapy and remained essentially the same six months later, according to Katherina Hauner, lead author and therapist of the study, which appears in Monday's Proceedings of the National Academy of Sciences.

[1] **arachnophobia:** a fear of spiders.

"These people had been clinically afraid of spiders since childhood . . . they'd have to leave the house if they thought there was a spider inside," she says. According to the NIH, about 8 percent of people have a "specific phobia," considered to be a "marked and persistent fear and avoidance of a specific object or situation."

Over the course of two hours, participants touched a live tarantula with a paintbrush, a gloved hand, and eventually their bare hand. "It's this idea that you slowly approach the thing you're afraid of. They learned that the spider was predictable and controllable, and by that time, they feel like it's not a spider anymore."

The study sheds light on the brain responses to fear and the changes that happen when a fear is overcome. Immediately after therapy, activity in the participants' amygdalas, the part of the brain believed to be responsible for fear responses, remained relatively **dormant** and stayed that way six months later when participants were exposed to spiders.

**dormant:**

2. REREAD AND DISCUSS Reread lines 1–22. With a small group, discuss whether the evidence convinces you that exposure therapy works. Cite facts and examples from the text to support your opinions.

3. READ As you read lines 23–35, continue to cite textual evidence.
   - Underline what happens in the brain during exposure therapy.
   - Circle the fears that exposure therapy treats best and underline the fears it does not treat.

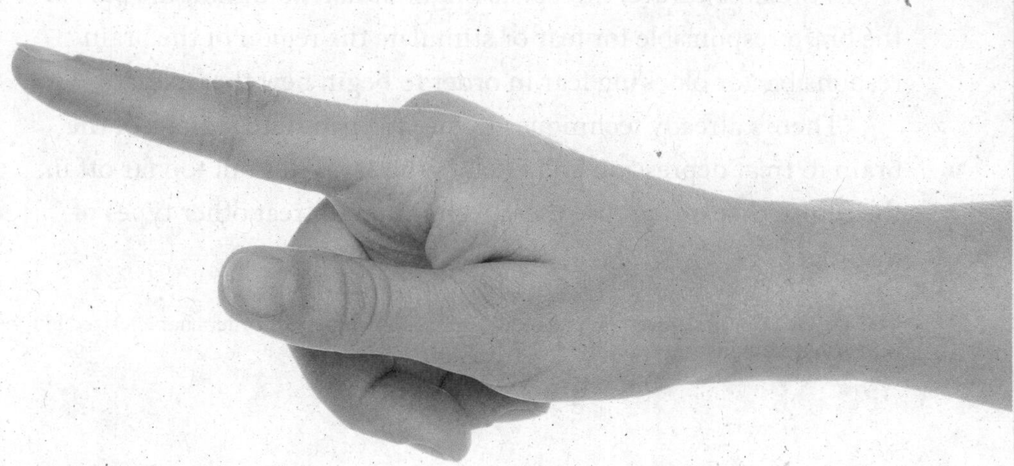

Hauner says the study proves that exposure therapy works and can potentially be used to develop new treatment methods for people with extreme phobias. She says a similar method can be used on people with fears of confined spaces, heights, flying, blood, and more.

"It has to be an **innocuous** object or situation—it's not a phobia if you're scared of sharks and don't want to go in shark-infested water," she says. "That's called being safe."

**innocuous:**

**4.** **REREAD** Reread lines 23–35. Summarize the study in lines 23–28 in your own words.

**5.** **READ** As you read lines 36–42, underline text that explains future uses of exposure therapy.

In the near future, therapists might be able to inhibit the part of the brain responsible for fear or stimulate the region of the brain responsible for blocking fear in order to begin new therapies.

stimulate:

"There's already techniques we use to **stimulate** regions of the brain to treat depression and OCD,"[2] she says. "It's not too far off in the future that we can use these techniques to treat other types of disorders."

[2] **OCD:** OCD, or obsessive-compulsive disorder, is an anxiety disorder characterized by intrusive thoughts and repetitive behaviors.

**6.** **REREAD** Reread lines 36–42. What is the main idea of this section?

## SHORT RESPONSE

*Cite Text Evidence* Which information from the text most convinces you of the effectiveness of exposure therapy? **Cite text evidence** with specific facts and examples from the text.

COLLECTION **2**

# Animal Intelligence

COLLECTION 2

# Animal Intelligence

"Each species, however inconspicuous and humble, . . . is a masterpiece."

—Edward O. Wilson


**SHORT STORY**
The Pod — **Maureen Crane Wartski**

**INFORMATIONAL TEXT**
Can Animals Feel and Think? — **DeShawn Jones**

**SCIENCE WRITING**
Bats! — **Mary Kay Carson**

**Background** **Maureen Crane Wartski** *was born in Ashiya, Japan, in 1940. Her European and Asian heritage and her deep connection with nature have strongly influenced her writing. In addition, Wartski is an accomplished artist. Like her writing, her watercolors often portray the natural world. Here she writes about dolphins, which, like whales, travel together in groups called "pods."*

# The Pod

Short Story by Maureen Crane Wartski

1. READ ▷ As you read lines 1–19, begin to collect and cite text evidence.
   - Circle the question at the beginning of the story.
   - In the margin, explain how the question helps you understand how Jesse feels about Pete at the beginning of the story.
   - Underline text that explains the reasons for Jesse's feelings about Pete and the rest of his family.

Couldn't Pete talk about anything but *fish*?

Jesse Waring tried to block his cousin's voice but there was no escape.

"Dolphins aren't fish, they're mammals," Pete was lecturing. "They look big and tough, but they can get stressed or scared, like the stranded dolphin we rescued. . . ."

"Jesse?" His mother was standing beside him, her eyes full of concern. His parents were always worrying about him these days. Jesse thought, **irritably**, and the other relatives were just as bad. *Poor Jesse, it's a shame about the accident. He used to be a great athlete. . . .* Even when they didn't talk to him, he could feel their pitying thoughts.

**irritably:**

"Can you go to the store for me?" his mother was saying. "We've run out of milk. That is," she added quickly, "if you're not too tired. . . ."

". . . And I want to make sure to visit the Cape Cod Stranding Network." Pete was droning on. "They have a hotline, and they do great work. . . ."

*Yada, yada, yada.* "Sure Mom," Jess said. *Anything to get away from Pete's lectures and all those pitying eyes.*

He snatched up car keys from the table in the entryway, grabbing his windbreaker as he limped out the door. Once outside, he wished he'd brought his parka—the wind had an icy sting—but he wasn't going back into the house.

He'd always enjoyed the annual Waring family reunion, when cousins, uncles and aunts from all over the country got together and rented a house on New England's Cape Cod, but this March was different. It was the first time the clan had gathered since the accident.

Jesse didn't want to think about how a man driving a pickup had jumped a red light, slamming into his car and fracturing his legs. Until then Jesse had been the star of the school soccer team, certain of an athletic scholarship.

"Not anymore," he muttered, then frowned as he realized he'd passed the store. Well, OK, there was a convenience store about 30 miles away, and the drive would give him some needed alone time.

At first, the silence was great.

But as Jesse drove on the road that wound beside the ocean, he kept thinking how his future had been smashed along with his legs. Pep talks that people gave him made it worse. He was a cripple, and

**2.** **◀ REREAD** Reread lines 7–14. How does Jesse respond to the accident? Explain what this tells you about his character. Support your answer with explicit textual evidence.

______________________________________________

______________________________________________

______________________________________________

______________________________________________

**3.** **READ ▶** As you read lines 20–40, continue to cite textual evidence.

- Underline the text that shows what Jesse was like before the accident.
- Note in the margin how this event has changed him.

he knew it. These days Jesse always felt as if there was a tight, hard knot in his chest.

On **impulse**, he turned the wheel, pulling into an empty parking lot that faced the water. He got out and limped down some stairs. Except for screeching seagulls and a few scattered rocks, the beach was deserted.

impulse:

Suddenly, Jesse tensed. *That rock . . . did it move?* He took a step closer and saw that it was no rock.

The dolphin wasn't very big, not even four feet long. When Jesse hobbled over, the big fish . . . *mammal,* according to Pete . . . rolled an eye at him. How long had it been there? It was breathing, but its sides were heaving painfully.

Fragments of Pete's endless **monologue** came back to him. His cousin had said that a dolphin's rib structure wasn't built to protect it on land. The body weight of this creature was slowly compressing its vital organs, and if it didn't get back into the water soon, it could die. It was going to low tide and the waves seemed far away. The best thing to do was to call Pete, who would know what to do. Jesse reached for his cell phone.

monologue:

It wasn't there. He'd left it in the pocket of his parka! He could drive home and get Pete, but that would mean leaving the dolphin.

4. **◀ REREAD** As you reread lines 28–35, compare Jesse's life before and after the accident. Why do you think he misses the convenience store? Support your answer with explicit textual evidence.

5. **READ ▶** As you read lines 41–61, continue to cite textual evidence.

- Underline the text that tells what Jesse thinks about immediately after he sees the stranded dolphin.
- Circle the text that shows how Jesse's feelings toward Pete have changed, and restate the change in the margin.

empathy:

arcing:

contraption:

Would it be alive when he got back? He knew nothing about this creature except that it was helpless.

The dolphin's eyes rolled again, and Jesse felt a sudden jolt of **empathy**.

It looked as scared as he had felt when they'd wheeled him into the emergency room that afternoon.

"Hey, Bud, . . ." Jesse knelt down beside the dolphin. "OK, I just can't leave you here to die. But how do I get you back into the water?"

Even if he managed to drag this creature that weighed — what? maybe 75 pounds? back into the water, the coarse sand might damage its skin. Jesse looked helplessly toward the gray ocean and was surprised to see dark shapes **arcing** out of the waves. A *pod*[1]—Pete's word—was out there.

"I think your family's waiting for you, Bud." Carefully, Jesse reached out and patted the dolphin. Was it his imagination that his touch made the dolphin calmer?

Jesse didn't want to waste time thinking about that. He was trying to remember what Pete had said about how, when he'd helped rescue a stranded dolphin, he had put the creature on a sort of blanket sling and carried that **contraption** down to the water. Well, he didn't have a blanket handy, so his windbreaker would have to do.

Carefully, Jesse scooped a hollow in the soft sand under the dolphin's head, then eased part of the windbreaker under it. He was streaming with sweat by the time he managed to maneuver as much of the dolphin as possible onto its makeshift "blanket," then began to drag the dolphin toward the water.

[1] **pod:** a school (or family) of dolphins or other sea mammals.

**6.** **REREAD AND DISCUSS** *Irony* is a contrast between what is expected and what actually happens. With a small group, discuss how Jesse's feelings about Pete's lectures may be changing. What makes this change surprising?

**7.** **READ** As you read lines 62–75, continue to cite textual evidence.

- Underline the text that demonstrates how Jesse continues to benefit from Pete's lecture as he cares for the dolphin.
- Circle the text that shows that Jesse is comparing himself to the dolphin.

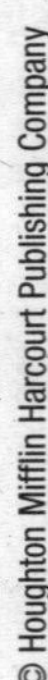

Twice, his legs buckled under him, tumbling him backward onto the sand, but he kept going until water was lapping around his ankles.

"Almost there, Bud," Jesse gritted.

As Jesse waded knee-deep into the water, the dolphin made some kind of noise and then began to swim.

"Woo hoo!" Jesse yelled, then yelped in **dismay**. The dolphin was swimming back toward the shore.

dismay:

What was wrong with the crazy creature? Pete's voice began to drone in Jesse's mind again, recounting his own dolphin rescue; *"The dolphin was* ***disoriented****. It kept heading for the shore. We had to guide it back into the deep water. . . ."*

disoriented:

Jesse waded deeper, past the breakers. Icy waves broke against him as he tried to head off the young dolphin. When he'd finally managed that, it wouldn't turn. He wished he had paid more attention to Pete's lecture, but wishing never helped.

Waves sent freezing spumes into his face. "Bud, you've got to save yourself." Jesse gritted through chattering teeth. "Nobody's going to do it for you. If you give up, you're finished. . . ."

Suddenly, as if it had at last understood, the young dolphin turned toward deeper water and began to swim toward the pod. Waiting dolphins arced nearer as if in welcome, and watching them, Jess thought of his own family. They'd be worried because he'd been gone so long.

*My* pod, he thought.

**8.** **◀ REREAD** Reread lines 66–75. What does Jesse do to care for the dolphin? How do his actions show that Jesse is changing as the story moves forward? Support your answer with explicit textual evidence.

______________________________________________

______________________________________________

______________________________________________

______________________________________________

**9.** **READ ▶** As you read lines 76–117, continue to cite textual evidence.

- Underline the actions Jesse takes to get the dolphin back into the water.
- In the margin, tell why it is ironic that Jesse remembers Pete's words.

He was freezing as he limped back to his car, but he was grinning, and he was happier than he'd been in a long while.

He was going to drive to the nearest store and call Pete, who would probably contact the Cape Cod Stranding Network hotline that he'd been talking about. The CCSN would make sure that Bud didn't strand again.

"But that's not going to happen anyway," Jesse said aloud.

He had a feeling the young dolphin was finally on the right track.

**10.** **REREAD** As you reread lines 101–117, explain why what Jesse says to the dolphin could really be applied to himself. To whom might Jesse be referring when he says that "the young dolphin is on the right track"?

## SHORT RESPONSE

*Cite Text Evidence* Explain how events in the story change Jesse's feelings about his cousin Pete. How does this response to Pete show that Jesse himself has changed as he struggled to rescue the stranded dolphin? **Cite text evidence** to support your response.

**Background** *For most of history, people have believed that animals are totally unlike human beings. A great scholar from the 1600s, René Descartes (dā kärt'), described animals as "machines"—incapable of thinking. In the early 1900s, the scientist Ivan Pavlov performed experiments that led many to believe that animals always acted predictably. In recent years, however, scientists have studied animal emotions and thought processes.*

# Can Animals Feel and Think?

Informational Text by DeShawn Jones

1. **READ ▶** As you read lines 1–13, begin to collect and cite text evidence.
   - Circle the central idea in the first paragraph, and underline the details that support the idea.
   - Circle the central idea in the second paragraph, and underline the supporting details.
   - In the margin, paraphrase each of the two central ideas.

Some people think that animals are just "animals," and that they have nothing in common with human beings. A growing body of scientific research, however, suggests otherwise. Most scientists now think that animals, especially mammals, can experience emotions. Other scientists take this a step further by saying that some animals actually think.

Think about what most dogs do when you scold them. They lower their heads and slink off to some secluded spot. Only when they sense that you are no longer angry do they come back out. On the other hand, when you return home after a day at school, your dog probably leaps around you, tail wagging furiously. But, do these reactions really indicate that dogs and other mammals feel emotions? They certainly seem to.

There are plenty of examples that seem to indicate that animals feel emotions such as fear, anger, joy, and grief. If the antelope did not feel fear, it would stand still or continue grazing instead of sprinting away at the sight of a cheetah. Mammals such as dolphins, chimpanzees, and rats show the feeling of joy in their love of playful activity. Elephants show signs of long-lasting grief when a member of the herd dies. Other mammals such as sea lions, bears, and moose also seem to become upset by a death in their group.

capacity:

Whether or not animals can actually think is a more difficult question. Do animals, for example, have the **capacity** to learn, solve problems, or guess what other animals are thinking? Research suggests that some animals can do this and more.

alliances:

resentment:

Chimpanzees in large captive colonies often cooperate with certain other chimpanzees in the colony. They have then been observed to suddenly switch **alliances** and seemingly double-cross each other. This behavior suggests that chimpanzees can, like humans, change their minds or feel **resentment**.

Pigs offer an interesting example of problem solving. A scientist from Bristol University discovered that stronger pigs looking for food would follow the lead of a weaker but smarter pig. The smarter pig would find the food. Then, the smarter pig would trick the stronger pig by distracting it. While the stronger pig wasn't looking, the smarter pig would dive in and gobble up the food.

**2.** **◀ REREAD** Write a summary of lines 1–13.

______________________________________________

______________________________________________

______________________________________________

______________________________________________

______________________________________________

**3.** **READ ▶** As you read lines 14–36, continue to cite textual evidence.

- Circle a sentence in lines 14–21 that informs the reader of the author's point of view.
- Underline at least one fact or example in each paragraph that supports the author's point of view.

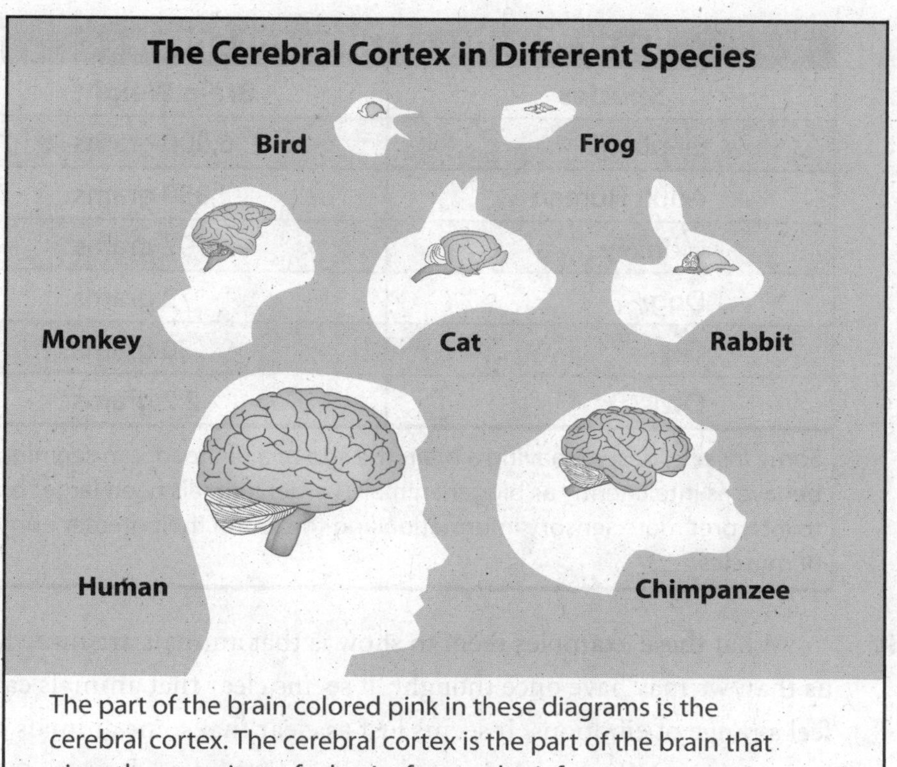


The part of the brain colored pink in these diagrams is the cerebral cortex. The cerebral cortex is the part of the brain that gives the capacity to feel pain, fear, and grief.

Perhaps the most amazing example of an animal thinking involves not a mammal, but a bird. Betty the crow makes her home in a laboratory in Oxford, England. She devised an **ingenious** solution for getting a treat in the form of food that scientists had inserted in a long tube. When she first tried to get the treat, she stuck her beak into the tube but found that the tube was too deep for her beak to reach the treat. Undaunted, she picked up a piece of wire that the scientists had placed beforehand in her cage. She bent the wire into a hook and used the hook to lift the treat from the tube. She did this not once, but repeatedly. What really amazed the scientists observing Betty was that she had never seen a piece of wire before. But this bird figured out the challenge, decided to use the wire, and then shape it into the perfect tool for getting the treat.

**ingenious:**

**4. READ ▶** As you read lines 37–53, continue to cite textual evidence.

- Circle the central idea in lines 37–49 and lines 50–53, and underline at least one detail that supports each central idea.
- In the margin, explain the author's purpose for including the diagram, chart, and captions.

| Brain Weights of Different Species | |
|---|---|
| **Species** | **Brain Weight** |
| Elephant | 6,000 grams |
| Adult Human | 1,350 grams |
| Monkey | 97 grams |
| Dog | 72 grams |
| Cat | 30 grams |
| Owl | 2.2 grams |

Some insects, despite having a brain the size of a pinhead, can seemingly behave as intelligently as bigger animals. Larger animals need larger brains to interpret more sensory information and to control their greater number of muscles.

What these examples seem to show is that animals are more like us than we may have once thought. It seems clear that animals can feel a range of emotions. It seems just as clear that some animals show an uncanny ability to do what appears to be "thinking."

5. **REREAD AND DISCUSS** Reread lines 37–53. With a small group, discuss whether the facts and examples the author cites provide sufficient support for his point of view. Be sure to consider the information presented in the diagram, chart, and captions.

## SHORT RESPONSE

*Cite Text Evidence* Write a summary of the article. Review your reading notes, and **cite text evidence** in your summary.

**Background** *Austin, Texas is home to millions of bats. It's also home to Bat Conservation International (BCI), an organization that works to conserve the world's bats and the environments where they live. In this excerpt from* The Bat Scientist, *nature writer Mary Kay Carson introduces Barbara French, a bat biologist who worked as science officer at BCI for 15 years. She now rescues and rehabilitates bats in Texas.*

# Bats!

Science Writing by Mary Kay Carson

CLOSE READ Notes

1. READ ▶ As you read lines 1–29, begin to collect and cite text evidence.
   - Circle facts about bats that make them different from humans.
   - Make notes in the margin about what happens to the bats after they have recovered in Barbara's care.

Barbara cares for a half-dozen or so different kinds of bats, including orphaned red bat babies, injured Mexican free-tailed bats, **recuperating** evening bats and yellow bats, captive straw-colored fruit bats, and an elderly cave bat. They're representatives of just a few of the world's thousand-plus bat species. Bats live on every continent except Antarctica. They come in all sizes—from as small as a hummingbird to as big as an owl. More than one-fifth of all five thousand or so mammal species are bats.

**recuperating:**

Flight is what makes bats unique. They became the only truly flying mammal more than 50 million years ago. The secret is their wings. Bat wings are made of naked skin over a framework of bones—the same bones we have. Barbara gently unfolds the wing of a Mexican free-tailed bat. "There's her elbow and her wrist," says Barbara as she touches the bones visible through the wing's thin skin.

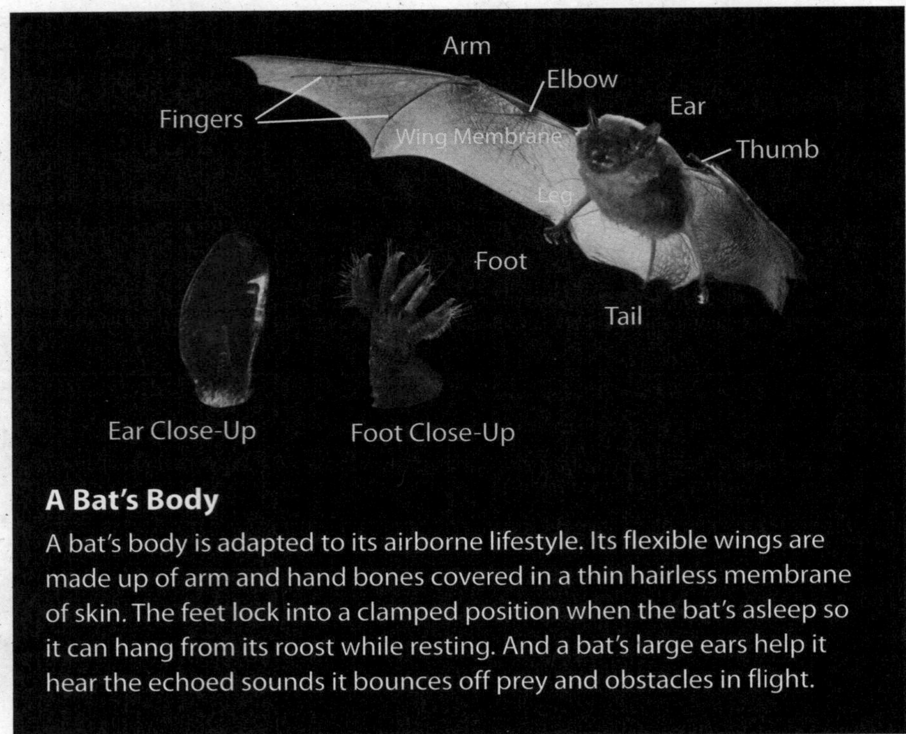


**A Bat's Body**

A bat's body is adapted to its airborne lifestyle. Its flexible wings are made up of arm and hand bones covered in a thin hairless membrane of skin. The feet lock into a clamped position when the bat's asleep so it can hang from its roost while resting. And a bat's large ears help it hear the echoed sounds it bounces off prey and obstacles in flight.

"And her thumb," she continues, pointing to the small nub[1] halfway down the top of the wing. Bats are master fliers. Their flapping wings propel them forward with speed and **maneuver** them around trees, after insects, and into crevices.[2]

**maneuver:**

When a bat can't fly, it's in trouble. Many of Barbara's bat patients have broken or hurt wings. "The wing injuries can often be treated," says Barbara. She sometimes does bat surgery, putting pins in the broken bones. "Finger injuries will heal well, but the upper arm is much harder," says Barbara. Only bats that can fly and catch insects on their own are released back into the wild. Outside the bat barn is a big flight cage where recuperating bats exercise and can catch bugs. When—and if—they can feed themselves, Barbara releases them back into the wild. Those that can't make it on their own become bat ambassadors, traveling with Barbara to events that teach people the truth about bats.

Bats are unique among mammals in other ways besides flight. In general, the bigger the mammal, the longer it lives. An elephant might live seventy years, a dog fifteen years, or a hamster only two years.

[1] **nub:** bump, bony protrusion.
[2] **crevices:** small gaps.

Bats break this rule. Even small bats can live forty or more years. For their size, bats are the longest-lived mammals on earth. Bats also reproduce slowly for their size. A mouse might have dozens of babies per year. Most kinds of bats give birth only once a year to a single pup. "One lost bat baby is a lost generation," says Barbara.

While the bat babies get milk, most adults in the bat barn eat live mealworms. "They're live beetle **larvae**," says Barbara. "I order eighty thousand mealworms a month." Most North American bats are insect-eaters. They have mouths full of sharp teeth to quickly crunch up insects as they fly. Each of the 1,100 different kinds of bats is especially adapted to the particular food it eats. Fruit-eating bats have big eyes and powerful noses to see and smell the ripe tropical fruit available year round. Nectar-eating bats also live in warm places with year-round flowers. They have long noses and tongues to reach deep into flowers and slurp up nectar. There are bats that snag fish with their strong-clawed feet, bats that catch birds in midair, and even bats that ambush mice on the ground! The infamous vampire bats of Central and South America drink the blood of mammals and birds.

**larvae:**

Most bats do their eating at night. They are nocturnal animals. So how do bats manage to fly around and find their food in the dark? Many fruit-eating bats have extra-big eyes, just like other nocturnal creatures. The African straw-colored fruit bats that Barbara cares for have dog-like faces—the reason these kinds of bats are often called flying foxes. "They depend on their eyesight and sense of smell to find fruit," explains Barbara.

**2.** **◀ REREAD** Reread lines 9–18. Underline the parts of a bat's body that humans also have. Study the image of the bat. How does showing body parts similar to a human's help you better understand a bat's body? Support your answer with explicit textual evidence.

______________________________________________

______________________________________________

______________________________________________

**3.** **READ ▶** As you read lines 30–85, continue to cite textual evidence.

- Underline text that explains how bats get food, including their use of sound.
- Make brief notes about echolocation in the margin.

Insect-eating bats are different. "Hearing is most important for them," says Barbara. "They can also smell and see, but echolocation is the biggest part of finding their food." These bats get around and hunt in the dark by "seeing" with sound.

Echolocation means locating something with echoes. Like sonar, it's a way to get information about something by bouncing sounds off it. Echolocating bats make loud calls and then listen for the echoes. The reflected sounds carry information about distance, speed, density, and size. A bat's brain turns the information into a kind of picture that helps the night-flying bat avoid trees, zero in on prey, and speed through caves. An echolocating bat "sees" its surroundings—caves, telephone poles, other bats, birds, and its prey—with sound. Bat echolocation is so precise that a bat can find a moth, tell how big it is, and know in which direction and at what speed it's moving, all in complete darkness. And it gathers all this information quickly enough to catch the moth while flying through a forest.

"It's why echolocators have such large ears," explains Barbara. Their big, sensitive ears collect the echoes like tiny satellite dishes. The strange faces of many bats are also echolocation tools. Those wrinkly lips and ears, leaf-shaped snouts called noseleafs, and bumpy foreheads focus the calls and echoes. Some bats even shout their calls through their megaphone-like nose. Bats are the loudest flying animals around! Their short calls or shouts are as loud as a smoke detector. Luckily for us, those echolocation calls are ultrasonic—too high pitched for humans to hear. So what is all the plainly heard chatter about inside Barbara's bat barn? "They're communicating," explains Barbara. Besides using ultrasonic calls to echolocate, bats use **audible** chirps, trills, buzzes, clicks, and purrs to talk to one another.

**audible:**

**4.** **◀ REREAD AND DISCUSS** Reread lines 51–61. In a small group, discuss the following question: If bats can see quite well, why is echolocation important to them?

**5.** **READ ▶** As you read lines 86–107 and the list of "Batty Myths" on page 34, continue to cite evidence.

- Underline ways that bats communicate with one another.
- Circle two ways that bats are important to their ecosystems.
- Underline three "batty" myths that you find surprising.

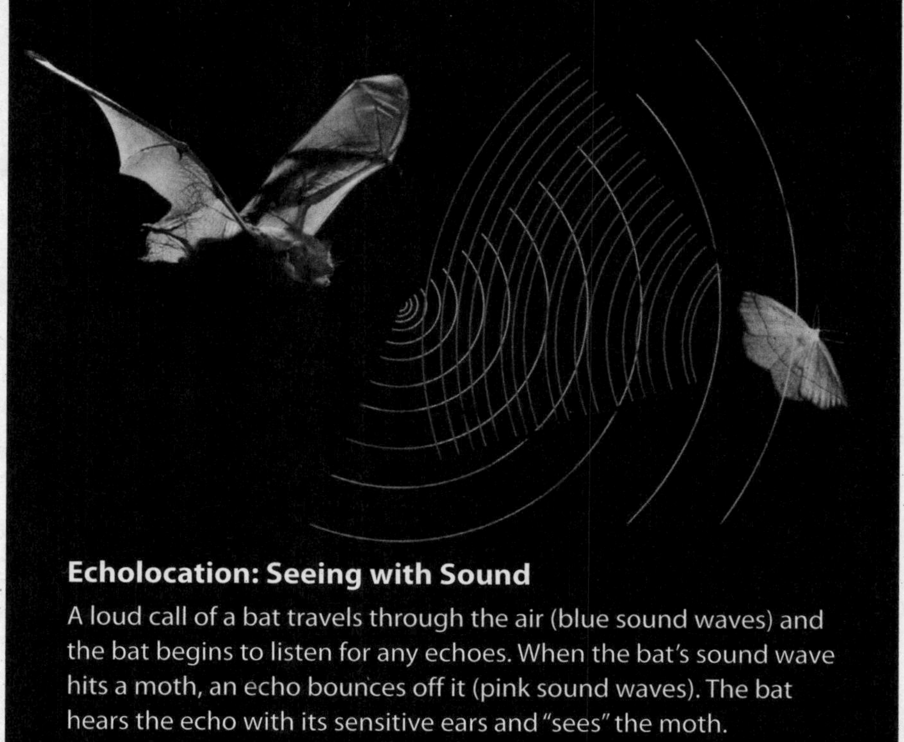

**Echolocation: Seeing with Sound**
A loud call of a bat travels through the air (blue sound waves) and the bat begins to listen for any echoes. When the bat's sound wave hits a moth, an echo bounces off it (pink sound waves). The bat hears the echo with its sensitive ears and "sees" the moth.

What do bats talk about? The normal stuff—food, friends, mates, territory, and complaints. The most talkative bats seem to be those that live in big colonies. Think of the mother bat coming home to Bracken Bat Cave after a night of hunting bugs. How does she find her pup among the millions of bats? One way she zeros in on her baby is by calling to it, and then the pup calls back to her. Barbara and other scientists have identified more than twenty different calls in Mexican free-tailed bats. Many were first discovered from studying the recorded conversations among the colony of fifty or so free-tailed bats in Barbara's barn. "They may even use a sort of grammar," says Barbara. "They put all of these little clicks and buzzes and trills together in certain ways to make certain meanings."

The fact that bats communicate with a complex language adds to what scientists are learning about these marvelous and misunderstood mammals. Though many people once scorned them as flying **vermin**, we now know that bats are intelligent, social, long-lived creatures more closely related to monkeys than mice. And no matter where they live or what they eat, each bat species plays an important role in its ecosystem. Bats are important controllers of insects. Fruit bats pollinate plants and spread seeds that grow forests. Cave-dwelling bats and the guano[3] they make support hundreds of unique cave species of insects, fungi,[4] and bacteria found no where else.

**vermin:**

[3] **guano:** the waste that bats produce.
[4] **fungi:** mushrooms.

## BATTY MYTHS

People still believe all kinds of crazy things about bats. Here are six of the most commonly misunderstood bat facts.

**Bats Are Not Blind.** All bats have eyes and can see quite well.

**Most Bats Do Not Have Rabies.** Like any wild animal, bats should not be touched, especially one found on the ground, which is more likely to be sick. However, getting rabies from a bat is very rare.

**Bats Do Not Get Tangled In People's Hair.** Bats are too good at flying for that— plus they generally avoid humans.

**Bats Do Not Suck Blood.** Not even the three species of vampire bats that live in Central and South America suck blood. They lap it up with their tiny tongues. No vampire bats live in the United States, except in zoos.

**primitive:**

**Bats Are Not Flying Mice.** DNA evidence shows that bats are not closely related to rodents. Some scientists believe they are more like **primitive** primates.

**Bats Are Not Pests In Need Of Extermination.** Bats can be safely removed from an attic or home without harming them. Bats are important pest controllers, often eating their own weight in pest insects every night.

6. REREAD Reread lines 86–97. Why might bats in big colonies be the most talkative?

## SHORT RESPONSE

*Cite Text Evidence* Explain how the information in the photos helps you understand the ways insect-eating bats communicate and find food. Be sure to **cite text evidence** in your response.

# COLLECTION 3

# Dealing with Disaster

COLLECTION **3**

# Dealing with Disaster

"Through every kind of disaster and setback and catastrophe. We are survivors."

—Robert Fulghum


**BOOK REVIEW**

## Moby-Duck

**David Holahan**

**SHORT STORY**

## There Will Come Soft Rains

**Ray Bradbury**

**NEWSPAPER ARTICLE**

## On the Titanic, Defined by What They Wore

**Guy Trebay**

**Background** *In 1992, a cargo ship departed from Hong Kong for Tacoma, Washington. During a storm, thousands of plastic bath toys called Friendly Floatees were washed overboard. Oceanographers later used these toys to study ocean currents. Some Floatees reached distant British shores more than ten years after the storm.*

# Moby-Duck

Book Review by David Holahan

**CLOSE READ** Notes

1. **READ ▶** As you read lines 1–31, begin to collect and cite evidence.
   - Underline what will happen to readers who read *Moby-Duck*.
   - In the margin, explain what the book's subtitle lets you know.
   - In the margin, summarize lines 19–31.

**intractable:**

Donovan Hohn's narrative about his monomaniacal[1] quest for the elusive yellow duck(s) bobbing somewhere upon the **intractable** oceans is more than a little Melvillian.[2] The plastic (not rubber) duckies that were cast so carelessly upon the waters are a symbol of our collective, all-consuming sin. Readers of this book will never again smile benignly at cloying little bath toys.

The plot of *Moby-Duck* (which has an epically long subtitle: "The True Story of 28,800 Bath Toys Lost at Sea and of the Beachcombers, Oceanographers, Environmentalists, and Fools, Including the Author, Who Went In Search of Them") revolves around the 1992 spill of 28,800 bathtub accessories from a massive container ship in the north Pacific, and the author's quest more than a decade later to track their

[1] **monomaniacal:** obsessed with one idea or subject.

[2] **Melvillian:** similar to the writings of author Herman Melville, specifically to the novel *Moby Dick*, the tale of a crew in search of a great white whale.

journey from China to purportedly pristine places like Hawaii and Alaska, and possibly through Northwest Passage to Maine. Will the author find one of these indestructible icons of domestic bliss on the bounding main, or along some secluded spit of sand, as other beachcombers have? Or will his odyssey end in failure, like that of the doomed Pequod?[3]

A former school teacher, Hohn got the idea for the book from a student's essay about the spill and toyed with the idea of writing about it from the safety of his home in New York City. His wife was expecting, after all. But he soon was consumed by the watery tale and the search for answers. So off he went, again and again. He would comb and help to clean up beaches in Alaska, which—despite being America's "Last Frontier"—is awash in startling amounts of debris: fishing gear, bottles, cans and the rest of the relentless plastic flotsam of our ever expanding civilization. The author also trolled for plastic on the high seas, shoved off with scientists studying oceanic currents, and booked a cruise on a container ship like the one that **disgorged** all those duckies (beavers, frogs, and turtles spilled, too, but these, clearly, are less **charismatic** commercial litter).

**disgorged:**

**charismatic:**

[3] **Pequod:** Captain Ahab's ship in Melville's novel *Moby Dick*.

**2.** REREAD Reread lines 19–31. Look up and define the words *debris* and *flotsam*. Use these words to explain where Hohn's search led him and what he found.

**3.** READ As you read lines 32–41, continue to cite text evidence.

- Underline what people once believed about the ocean.
- Study the map showing where ocean currents carried the shipwrecked toys.
- Underline information about the Great Pacific Garbage Patch in the text and in the caption.

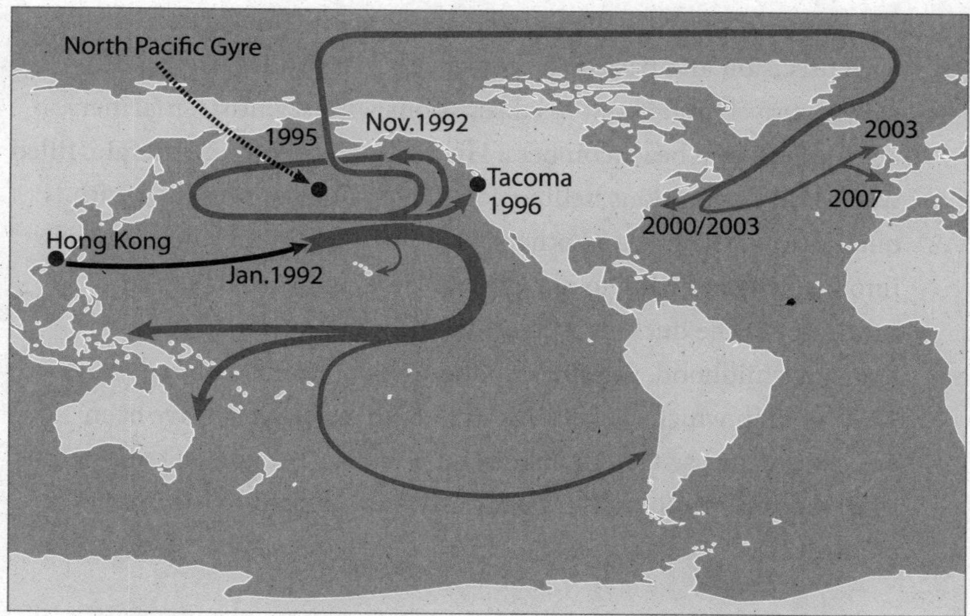


This map shows where the Floatees traveled between the time they went overboard in 1992 and 2007. Two thousand of the Floatees, along with the Great Pacific Garbage Patch, are stuck in the circular currents of the North Pacific Gyre.

Cleaning up a remote beach where grizzly bears forage is hardly the answer to plastic pollution, it turns out. The shoreline will be well littered again in no time. And where does that leave the oceans, where our floating industrial waste stream often is aggregated by the currents into places with names like the Great Pacific Garbage Patch? The oceans were once thought to be too vast for us to properly befoul—even Rachel Carson[4] thought as much for a time. The Great Pacific Garbage Patch is roughly the size of Texas and growing, and plastic has become as common as plankton in many places. Birds and fish mistake the smaller portions for food.

[4] **Rachel Carson:** American conservationist, scientist, ecologist, and marine biologist; often credited with being the founder of the environmental movement.

4. **◀ REREAD AND DISCUSS** Review lines 32–41 and the map. With a small group, integrate information from the text and the map to explain the many effects of a single cause: the spill of 28,000 bathtub toys.

5. **READ ▶** As you read lines 42–54, continue to cite text evidence. Underline the descriptive words and phrases Holahan uses to describe Hohn's writing.

ken:

Hohn, who is now the features editor at GQ [magazine], writes with precision and passion about what he sees and learns on his various travels and about his discussions with scientists, mariners, do-gooders, and beachcombers. His writing is lively and literate, filled with vivid descriptions, telling context, and lightly seasoned with quotes from Melville and others. He knows a symbol when one bobs into his **ken**, and what to do with it: "Here, then, is one of the meanings of the duck. It represents this vision of childhood—the hygienic childhood, the safe childhood, the brightly colored childhood in which everything, even bathtub articles, have been designed to please the childish mind, much as the golden fruit in that most famous origin myth of paradise 'was pleasant to the eyes' of childish Eve."

**6.** **◀ REREAD** Reread lines 42–54. Is this a positive or negative review of Hohn's book? Cite evidence from the text to support your answer.

**7.** **READ ▶** As you read lines 55–78, continue to cite text evidence.

- Circle environmental "cons" and underline real solutions to reducing the amount of trash in the ocean.
- Explain in the margin what the technique of "greenwashing" means. Be sure to read the footnote that defines the term.

"So what is the answer to oceans beset by a rising tide of indestructible trash?"

The author also knows a clever con when he sees one. He concludes that "Keep America Beautiful" approaches, which are largely spawned and bankrolled by the very corporations that are producing all the plastic detritus, are not the answer. There is no way to keep much of anything beautiful when barely five percent of all plastic we use is recycled. The whole point of plastic things is that they are made to be thrown away; that's what makes them so darn consumer-friendly and profitable. What companies are doing with their "Let's Not Litter" PR is to "greenwash"[5] their own sizeable and systemic culpability, according to Hohn.

So what is the answer to oceans beset by a rising tide of indestructible trash? One is people like boat captain Charlie Moore, a self-made scientist and activist, who works to raise public awareness of the problem and lobbies for more enlightened regulations and corporate practices. Others Hohn encounters are volunteering their time and money to clean up our collective mess.

[5] **greenwashing:** a practice in which a company deceptively promotes the idea that its product is good for the environment when that is not the case.

But the author wonders if such solutions, nibbling around the edges, are enough: "I'd like to share Moore's faith in the arc of progress . . . but I had a hard time imagining the bright future he saw, in which we Americans would trade conspicuous consumption for cradle-to-cradle manufacturing practices, disposable plastics for zero-waste policies and closed ecological loops. I had a hard time because such a future seemed to me **inimical** to the American gospel of perpetual economic growth."

**inimical:**

**8.** REREAD Reread lines 55–78. Summarize why certain actions are "cons," according to Hohn.

## SHORT RESPONSE

*Cite Text Evidence* At the beginning of this review, Holahan says that "Readers of this book will never again smile" at "little bath toys" again. Do you agree or disagree with this statement, now that you know about the life of the Floatees? Support your response by **citing text evidence.**

**Background** Ray Bradbury *(1920–2012) was born in a small town named Waukegan, Illinois. He was hired to write short stories for a radio show at the age of 14 and joined the Los Angeles Science Fiction Society at the age of 16. In 1953, he published his most famous book,* Fahrenheit 451, *which warned of the dangers of book censorship. In all, Ray Bradbury wrote 27 novels and over 600 short stories.*

# There Will Come Soft Rains

Short Story by Ray Bradbury

1. **READ ▶** As you read lines 1–15, begin to collect and cite evidence.
   - Underline examples of personification in the text.
   - In the margin, define "voice-clock," using clues from the text.
   - Circle two phrases that help you infer that no people are in the house.

In the living room the voice-clock sang, *Ticktock, seven o'clock, time to get up, time to get up, seven o'clock!* as if it were afraid that nobody would. The morning house lay empty. The clock ticked on, repeating and repeating its sounds into the emptiness. *Seven-nine, breakfast time, seven-nine!*

In the kitchen the breakfast stove gave a hissing sigh and ejected from its warm interior eight pieces of perfectly browned toast, eight eggs sunny side up, sixteen slices of bacon, and two coffees.

"Today is August 4, 2026," said a second voice from the kitchen ceiling, "in the city of Allendale, California." It repeated the date three times for memory's sake. "Today is Mr. Featherstone's birthday. Today is the anniversary of Tilita's marriage. Insurance is payable, as are the water, gas, and light bills."

Somewhere in the walls, relays clicked, memory tapes glided under electric eyes.

*Eight-one, tick-tock, eight-one o'clock, off to school, off to work, run, run, eight-one!* But no doors slammed, no carpets took the soft tread of rubber heels. It was raining outside. The weather box on the front door sang quietly: "Rain, rain, go away; rubbers, raincoats for today . . . " And the rain tapped on the empty house, echoing.

Outside, the garage chimed and lifted its door to reveal the waiting car. After a long wait the door swung down again.

At eight-thirty the eggs were shriveled and the toast was like stone. An aluminum wedge scraped them into the sink, where hot water whirled them down a metal throat which digested and flushed them away to the distant sea. The dirty dishes were dropped into a hot washer and emerged twinkling dry.

*Nine-fifteen,* sang the clock, *time to clean.*

warrens:

Out of **warrens** in the wall, tiny robot mice darted. The rooms were acrawl with the small cleaning animals, all rubber and metal. They thudded against chairs, whirling their moustached runners, kneading the rug nap, sucking gently at hidden dust. Then, like mysterious invaders, they popped into their burrows. Their pink electric eyes faded. The house was clean.

*Ten o'clock.* The sun came out from behind the rain. The house stood alone in a city of rubble and ashes. This was the one house left standing. At night the ruined city gave off a radioactive glow which could be seen for miles.

**2.** **◀ REREAD** Reread lines 1–15. What kind of "personality" does the house have? Support your answer with explicit textual evidence.

**3.** **READ ▶** As you read lines 16–38, continue to cite text evidence.

- Underline examples of personification in the text.
- In the margin, explain what the author is referring to when he says "a metal throat."
- Circle what makes the city visible for miles.

*Ten-fifteen.* The garden sprinklers whirled up in golden founts, filling the soft morning air with scatterings of brightness. The water pelted windowpanes, running down the charred west side where the house had been burned evenly free of its white paint. The entire west face of the house was black, save for five places. Here the silhouette in paint of a man mowing a lawn. Here, as in a photograph, a woman bent to pick flowers. Still farther over, their images burned on wood in one titanic instant, a small boy, hands flung into the air; higher up, the image of a thrown ball, and opposite him a girl, hands raised to catch a ball which never came down.

The five spots of paint—the man, the woman, the children, the ball—remained. The rest was a thin charcoaled layer.

The gentle sprinkler rain filled the garden with falling light.

Until this day, how well the house had kept its peace. How carefully it had inquired, "Who goes there? What's the password?" and, getting no answer from lonely foxes and whining cats, it had shut up its windows and drawn shades in an old-maidenly preoccupation with self-protection which bordered on a mechanical **paranoia.**

**paranoia:**

It quivered at each sound, the house did. If a sparrow brushed a window, the shade snapped up. The bird, startled, flew off! No, not even a bird must touch the house!

**4.** **REREAD** Reread lines 35–38. What conclusion can you draw from the text about what happened to the rest of the houses in the town?

**5.** **READ** As you read lines 39–59, continue to cite text evidence.

- Underline examples of personification in the text.
- In the margin, explain what the boy and girl were doing when the nuclear event occurred.
- Circle the sentence that lets you know something bad is about to happen to the house.

CLOSE READ
Notes

The house was an altar with ten thousand attendants, big, small, servicing, attending, in choirs. But the gods had gone away, and the ritual of the religion continued senselessly, uselessly.

*Twelve noon.*

A dog whined, shivering, on the front porch.

The front door recognized the dog voice and opened. The dog, once huge and fleshy, but now gone to bone and covered with sores, moved in and through the house, tracking mud. Behind it whirred angry mice, angry at having to pick up mud; angry at inconvenience.

For not a leaf fragment blew under the door but what the wall panels flipped open and the copper scrap rats flashed swiftly out. The offending dust, hair, or paper, seized in miniature steel jaws, was raced back to the burrows. There, down tubes which fed into the cellar, it was dropped into the sighing vent of an incinerator which sat like evil Baal[1] in a dark corner.

The dog ran upstairs, hysterically yelping to each door, at last realizing, as the house realized, that only silence was here.

It sniffed the air and scratched the kitchen door. Behind the door, the stove was making pancakes which filled the house with a rich baked odor and the scent of maple syrup.

The dog frothed at the mouth, lying at the door, sniffing, its eyes turned to fire. It ran wildly in circles, biting at its tail, spun in a frenzy, and died. It lay in the parlor for an hour.

*Two o'clock,* sang a voice.

Delicately sensing decay at last, the regiments of mice hummed out as softly as blown gray leaves in an electrical wind.

[1] **Baal:** In the Bible, the god of Canaan, whom the Israelites came to recognize as a false god.

6. **REREAD AND DISCUSS** Reread lines 39–50. In a small group, discuss what conclusions you can draw about the nuclear event, based on the silhouettes, or outlines, on the side of the house.

7. **READ** As you read lines 60–96, continue to cite text evidence.
   - Underline examples of personification in the text.
   - In the margin, explain who the attendants and gods are.
   - In the margin, explain why the dog yelps at each door.

*Two-fifteen.*

The dog was gone.

In the cellar, the incinerator glowed suddenly and a whirl of sparks leaped up the chimney.

*Two thirty-five.*

Bridge[2] tables sprouted from patio walls. Playing cards fluttered onto pads in a shower of pips.[3] Martinis manifested on an oaken bench with egg-salad sandwiches. Music played.

But the tables were silent and the cards untouched.

At four o'clock the tables folded like great butterflies back through the paneled walls.

---

[2] **bridge:** a card game.

[3] **pips:** symbols on the front of a playing card that denote the suit.

**8.** **◀ REREAD** Reread lines 65–89. What inferences can you make about what killed the dog? What happens to the dog's body after it dies? Cite textual evidence to support your inference.

> "The voice said at last, 'Since you express no preference, I shall select a poem at random.'"

*Four-thirty.*

The nursery walls glowed. Animals took shape: yellow giraffes, blue lions, pink antelopes, lilac panthers cavorting in crystal substance. The walls were glass. They looked out upon color and fantasy. Hidden films clocked through well-oiled sprockets, and the walls lived. The nursery floor was woven to resemble a crisp cereal meadow. Over this ran aluminum roaches and iron crickets, and in the hot, still air butterflies of delicate red tissue wavered among the sharp aromas of animal spoors! There was the sound like a great matted yellow hive of bees within a dark bellows, the lazy bumble of a purring lion. And there was the patter of okapi[4] feet and the murmur of a fresh jungle rain, like other hoofs, falling upon the summer-starched grass. Now the walls dissolved into distances of parched weed, mile on mile, and warm endless sky. The animals drew away into thorn brakes[5] and water holes.

It was the children's hour.

*Five o'clock.* The bath filled with clear hot water.

*Six, seven, eight o'clock.* The dinner dishes manipulated like magic tricks, and in the study a *click*. In the metal stand opposite the hearth

---

[4] **okapi:** an animal, similar to a giraffe, with zebra striping.

[5] **thorn brakes:** clumps of thorns; thickets.

**9.** **READ ▶** As you read lines 97–140, continue to cite text evidence.

- Underline examples of personification in the text.
- In the margin, explain why "not one will know of the war" (line 132).
- Circle evidence that helps you infer that the animals are not real.

where a fire now blazed up warmly, a cigar popped out, half an inch of soft gray ash on it, smoking, waiting.

*Nine o'clock.* The beds warmed their hidden circuits, for nights were cool here.

*Nine-five.* A voice spoke from the study ceiling:

"Mrs. McClellan, which poem would you like this evening?"

The house was silent.

The voice said at last, "Since you express no preference, I shall select a poem at random." Quiet music rose to back the voice. "Sara Teasdale. As I recall, your favorite. . . .

*There will come soft rains and the smell of the ground,*
*And swallows circling with their shimmering sound;*

*And frogs in the pools singing at night,*
*And wild plum trees in **tremulous** white;*

*Robins will wear their feathery fire,*
*Whistling their whims on a low fence-wire;*

*And not one will know of the war, not one*
*Will care at last when it is done.*

*Not one would mind, neither bird nor tree,*
*If mankind perished utterly;*

*And Spring herself, when she woke at dawn*
*Would scarcely know that we were gone."*

The fire burned on the stone hearth, and the cigar fell away into a mound of quiet ash on its tray. The empty chairs faced each other between the silent walls, and the music played.

At ten o'clock the house began to die.

The wind blew. A falling tree bough crashed through the kitchen window. Cleaning solvent, bottled, shattered over the stove. The room was ablaze in an instant!

**tremulous:**

**10.** **◀ REREAD AND DISCUSS** Reread lines 126–137. The title of this poem is "There Will Come Soft Rains." In a small group, discuss why Bradbury might have borrowed this title for his story.

**11.** **READ ▶** As you read lines 141–189, continue to cite evidence.

- Underline examples of personification in the text.
- In the margin, explain what the "twenty snakes" are.
- Circle the names of parts of the body.

"Fire!" screamed a voice. The house lights flashed, water pumps shot water from the ceilings. But the solvent spread on the linoleum, licking, eating, under the kitchen door, while the voices took it up in chorus: "Fire, fire, fire!"

The house tried to save itself. Doors sprang tightly shut, but the windows were broken by the heat and the wind blew and sucked upon the fire.

The house gave ground as the fire in ten billion angry sparks moved with flaming ease from room to room and then up the stairs. While scurrying water rats squeaked from the walls, pistoled their water, and ran for more. And the wall sprays let down showers of mechanical rain.

But too late. Somewhere, sighing, a pump shrugged to a stop. The quenching rain ceased. The reserve water supply which had filled baths and washed dishes for many quiet days was gone.

The fire crackled up the stairs. It fed upon Picassos and Matisses in the upper halls, like delicacies, baking off the oily flesh, tenderly crisping the canvases into black shavings.

Now the fire lay in beds, stood in windows, changed the colors of drapes!

And then, reinforcements.

From attic trapdoors, blind robot faces peered down with faucet mouths gushing green chemical.

The fire backed off, as even an elephant must at the sight of a dead snake. Now there were twenty snakes whipping over the floor, killing the fire with a clear cold venom of green froth.

But the fire was clever. It had sent flame outside the house, up through the attic to the pumps there. An explosion! The attic brain which directed the pumps was shattered into bronze shrapnel on the beams.

The fire rushed back into every closet and felt of the clothes hung there.

The house shuddered, oak bone on bone, its bared skeleton cringing from the heat, its wire, its nerves revealed as if a surgeon had

torn the skin off to let the red veins and capillaries quiver in the scalded air. Help, help! Fire! Run, run! Heat snapped mirrors like the first brittle winter ice. And the voices wailed, Fire, fire, run, run, like a tragic nursery rhyme, a dozen voices, high, low, like children dying in a forest, alone, alone. And the voices fading as the wires popped their sheathings like hot chestnuts. One, two, three, four, five voices died.

In the nursery the jungle burned. Blue lions roared, purple giraffes bounded off. The panthers ran in circles, changing color, and ten million animals, running before the fire, vanished off toward a distant steaming river. . . .

Ten more voices died. In the last instant under the fire avalanche, other choruses, **oblivious,** could be heard announcing the time, playing music, cutting the lawn by remote-control mower, or setting an umbrella frantically out and in, the slamming and opening front door, a thousand things happening, like a clock shop when each clock strikes the hour insanely before or after the other, a scene of maniac confusion, yet unity; singing, screaming, a few last cleaning mice darting bravely out to carry the horrid ashes away! And one voice, with **sublime** disregard for the situation, read poetry aloud in the fiery study, until all the film spools burned, until all the wires withered and the circuits cracked.

**oblivious:**

**sublime:**

The fire burst the house and let it slam flat down, puffing out skirts of spark and smoke.

In the kitchen, an instant before the rain of fire and timber, the stove could be seen making breakfasts at a psychopathic rate, ten dozen eggs, six loaves of toast, twenty dozen bacon strips, which, eaten by fire, started the stove working again, hysterically hissing!

**12.** **◀ REREAD AND DISCUSS** Reread lines 149–185. In a small group, discuss the ways in which the "personalities" of the fire and the house create an impression of war.

**13.** **READ ▶** As you read lines 190–216, continue to cite text evidence.

- Underline examples of personification.
- In the margin, describe two actions that happen at both the beginning and the end of the story.

The crash. The attic smashing into kitchen and parlor. The parlor into cellar, cellar into subcellar. Deep freeze, armchair, film tapes, circuits, beds, and all like skeletons thrown in a cluttered mound deep under.

Smoke and silence. A great quantity of smoke.

Dawn showed faintly in the east. Among the ruins, one wall stood alone. Within the wall, a last voice said, over and over again and again, even as the sun rose to shine upon the heaped rubble and steam:

"Today is August 5, 2026, today is August 5, 2026, today is . . ."

**14.** **REREAD AND DISCUSS** Reread lines 212–216. In a small group, discuss your responses to the ending. What is ironic, or unexpected, about the way the story ends?

## SHORT RESPONSE

*Cite Text Evidence* What overall effect does the author's personification of the house have on the reader as the house burns down? **Cite text evidence** to support your ideas.

**Background** *On April 10th, 1912, the RMS* Titanic *left Southampton, England, for New York City on its first and only voyage. The* Titanic *had been called "unsinkable" and was the most luxurious passenger liner of its day. On April 15th, the ship collided with an iceberg and sank. Over 1,500 people died in the freezing waters. The wreckage was discovered in 1985, but the ship remains on the ocean floor to this day. The* Titanic *has been immortalized through film, books, television series, songs, exhibits—and in this recent newspaper article.*

# On the Titanic, Defined by What They Wore

## Newspaper Article by Guy Trebay

1. READ ▶ As you read lines 1–34, begin to cite text evidence.
   - In the margin, explain what you think the article's title means.
   - In the margin, paraphrase what the second sentence says.
   - Underline items recovered from the *Titanic*.

Tatters and scraps, they emerged from the deep coated with mire and miraculously although tenuously intact. Treated with the reverence due relics of perhaps the greatest maritime tragedy and with all the care modern conservation science could summon, they were restored, put on display and then offered this week in an exceptional single-lot auction of the more than 5,000 objects (with a current estimated worth of $190 million) that salvagers of the Titanic found scattered across the North Atlantic seabed.

A surprising amount of ephemera[1] defied logic to survive the sinking of the unsinkable ocean liner that went to the bottom 100 years ago on April 15.

Most astonishing of all the recovered items, it would seem, were the articles of clothing either carried or worn by passengers before the 882-foot-long liner sank in icy water. The ship broke apart and shot to

[1] **ephemera:** things that are useful for only a short time.

the bottom; its contents fell more slowly, fluttering to the depths like grim leaf fall.

And there, in the lightless saline netherworld, a vest, a trilby hat, a pair of laced boots, a belted valise and an alligator bag (along with a huge range of artifacts) lay scattered across a broad apron of remnants.

expedition:

The wreck was discovered in 1985 and the objects were brought to the surface over the course of seven **expeditions.** Perhaps more than the teacups or perfume flacons, the garments eerily conjure lives lost that clear April night, so much so that when the Academy Award-winning designer Deborah L. Scott prepared to create costumes for James Cameron's blockbuster 1997 film "Titanic," she covered her office walls with photographs of the Titanic's passengers to absorb the sartorial[2] elements that enliven character.

The removable celluloid collars with laundry marks inside, the man's vest with a single vertical buttonhole for a watch chain and fob, the homespun finery packed away by village girls as a trousseau[3] for an imaginary future: these sorts of detail were employed by Ms. Scott to summon the beings who once inhabited garments that in some cases, though it is hard to imagine, survived their owners.

Consider, for instance, Marion Meanwell's handbag.

Using public records, newspaper accounts at the time and the recollections of survivors, historians like Richard Davenport-Hines, author of "Voyagers of the Titanic: Passengers, Sailors, Shipbuilders,

[2] **sartorial:** related to clothing.
[3] **trousseau:** a bride's personal possessions.

2. **◀ REREAD** Reread lines 21–34. Where did Deborah L. Scott find inspiration for her costume designs for the 1997 movie?

3. **READ ▶** As you read lines 35–80, continue to cite text evidence.
- In the margin, paraphrase the quote at the top of the next page.
- Underline information that helps you understand Mrs. Meanwell's story.
- In the margin, explain why it was so important to have credentials.

**"As was true of many ocean voyagers of the time, Mrs. Meanwell was on a passage intended to be a momentous alteration of a settled life."**

Aristocrats, and the Worlds They Came From," have pieced together fragmentary biographies of victims like Mrs. Meanwell (nee Ogden), a British milliner[4] traveling aboard the Titanic on a third-class ticket.

As was true of many ocean voyagers of the time, Mrs. Meanwell was on a passage intended to be a momentous alteration of a settled life. First chartered to sail on the liner Majestic, Mrs. Meanwell rebooked on the Titanic after that vessel was removed from regular service. Tucked into her handbag were a number of documents, among them a letter from the London landlords Wheeler Sons & Co.

This **innocuous** note, stating blandly that "we have always found Meanwell a good tenant and prompt in payment of her rent," carried an extra freight of meaning for an immigrant hoping to build a new life.

**innocuous:**

"If you were coming over without **credentials** or with no prospect of work," Mr. Davenport-Hines said, it was not uncommon for examiners at Ellis Island to refuse entry to new arrivals and to send them home as "vagrants or tramps."

**credentials:**

Then as now, an alligator bag was a luxury item, a satchel of substance carried by a woman whose own social authority it advertised. Mrs. Meanwell was parted from her alligator bag on the night the Titanic sank and, while she perished, her purse did not.

[4] **milliner:** hatmaker.

"Inside it was her marriage license, as well as her parents' wedding license," said David Galusha, a conservator for Premier Exhibition, the Atlanta-based company that sold the Titanic relics, along with the video archives of its salvage expeditions and the intellectual rights to create objects using the R.M.S. Titanic "brand."

"She had sold everything, was a widow and was moving to the United States to be with her daughter, who had two children, to assist with them," Mr. Galusha said of Mrs. Meanwell.

That the bag survived was owed in part to the fact that the objects scattered from the wreck spent the last century, "two miles down, in an environment with no light, and hardly any oxygen," the conservator said. There was something else. "The thickness of the alligator skin, the quality, is no comparison to what you would find today," Mr. Galusha said. "There was a general attitude at the time of making things durable, things that would stand the test of time."

That they did so is an unexpectedly moving aspect of a tale so often rehearsed that its human dimensions are sometimes overlooked. "Titanic" may be, as some claim, one of the most universally recognized names in the English language. Yet the lives at the heart of the story are easily forgotten, transformed into facile metaphors and symbols of gender and class.

**4.** **◀ REREAD** Reread lines 42–80. Why does the author include the narrative history about Mrs. Meanwell? Cite text evidence in your response.

**5.** **READ ▶** As you read lines 81–114, continue to cite text evidence.

- Underline the role that clothing played after the *Titanic* sank.
- In the margin, explain what the names of first-class passengers reveal about the gap between social classes.
- In the margin, paraphrase what Cohen says about the *Titanic* as a stage.

> **"The Titanic was this stage where people were performing certain versions of themselves, for all kinds of audiences."**

There is the tragic noblesse of the first-class passengers, people named Straus and Widener and Guggenheim; the hopeless scrabbling of the businessmen and boys traveling in second class, some kept at gunpoint from entering lifeboats that went off half-filled; and the wretched doom of those nameless victims at the bottom of the social scale.

"They were all judged finally on their clothes and the quality of their clothes," Mr. Davenport-Hines said, adding that among the aspects of the story most laden with pathos is the contemporary depiction of bodies frozen into life jackets and hauled from the North Atlantic and sorted by class, largely according to what else they had on.

Clothes, said Lisa Cohen, a biographer whose book "All We Know" delineates the lives of three early modernist women—Mercedes de Acosta, Madge Garland, Esther Murphy—in part by using the "soft history" of fashion to demonstrate that our surfaces **elucidate** "our depths," as the author said.

**elucidate:**

The identity masquerade that artists like Cindy Sherman explore to theatrical effect was on prominent view aboard the floating theater of an ocean passage, Ms. Cohen said. The Titanic was in that sense a stage prop moving across what was by all accounts a flat and unthreatening ocean and also across the proscenium[5] of a new century.

"The Titanic was this stage where people were performing certain versions of themselves, for all kinds of audiences," Ms. Cohen said. "It was a transitional space in a transitional period, a time of self-invention right before the war."

[5] **proscenium:** the part of the stage in front of the curtain.

An overlay of markings has here been applied to the original *Olympic/Titanic* plan from *The Shipbuilder* to compare the present condition of the wreck to the ship as her builders conceived her.

1 Rudder buried 45 feet.
2 Poop Deck peeled back over stern.
3 After Well Deck torn away.
4 Decks collapsed and compressed.
5 Starboard A-Deck cargo crane wrenched but still fitted.
6 Second-class entrance and elevator housing remain.
7 Decks collapsed down.
8 Deck rests on cylinder heads of reciprocating engines.

**nuanced:**

Fixed and flattened in memory by the shock of disaster, the realities of the Titanic become available to **nuanced** interpretation only now, a century later, just as with the sale this week of the hats and vests and shoes and watches saved from the ocean, come into wider view.

"It's the power of the surface that's so beautiful here," Ms. Cohen said. "The smallest detail reveals so much."

At a minimum, the sartorial details convey some overlooked information: people were generally smaller in 1912, had tidier heads, more-compact torsos, less-capacious lungs.

**6.** **REREAD AND DISCUSS** Reread lines 98–114. With a small group, discuss the many ways in which the *Titanic* was a "stage." In what ways were the passengers' clothing like costumes?

**7.** **READ** As you read lines 115–148, continue to cite text evidence.

- Circle two examples of recovered clothing.
- In the margin, explain what the recovered clothing teaches about people of the past.
- Underline text that shows how people—on screen and in real life—make a statement with clothing.

9 Shell plating remains partially upright although Boat Deck is angled down in center.

10 One-foot gap in expansion joint.

11 Hull buckled below expansion joint.

12 Possible iceberg damage here.

13 Bow angled downward.

14 Buckling caused by angle of bow.

15 Level of original keel.

16 Bow plowed in over 60 feet.

"Take the trilby," Mr. Galusha, the conservator, said, referring to a felt hat that emerged from conservation in such pristine condition that "it could literally be worn right now," although only by a woman with a small head.

"There's a C.S.I.[6] side of this story," he said. The size of the hat tacitly points to shifts in diet over the last century, to the introduction of antibiotics and vitamins. "On average, the size of our rib cages increases 4 percent per generation," Mr. Galusha said, a claim that would go a long way toward explaining why the contemporary bride can't fit into her grandmother's wedding gown.

People were frugal in 1912, or anyway less accustomed to the ease of disposable fashion. A patch of "invisible" weaving can still be detected in a custom-made gentleman's suit recovered from the Titanic wreckage. "It was a good suit, and instead of discarding the trousers, the owner had the hole repaired," Mr. Galusha said.

[6] **C.S.I.:** Crime Scene Investigation.



**8.** **REREAD AND DISCUSS** Review the diagram of the *Titanic*. With a small group, discuss what the diagram shows.

Though they largely passed into legend, those who lost their lives in the epoch-making shipwreck were never "characters," said Deborah Nadoolman Landis, the curator of "Hollywood Costume," an exhibition exploring the role costume design plays in cinema history that will open in October at the Victoria and Albert Museum in London. "A character is a pretend person, and real people lost their lives," in the wreck of the Titanic, said Ms. Landis, an Academy Award-nominated designer. On-screen, their clothes served a crucial function, as flashcard symbols of social identity. "One of the ways you make people real in movies is through clothes."

amalgam:

People are to a surprising extent what they imagine themselves to be every time they get dressed, Ms. Landis said. "Our clothing is an **amalgam** of what we are: the shoes, the vest, the trousers, the suit jacket purchased at different times," she said. "Clothes hold us together in so many ways. They're the closest thing to our bodies, our pulse."

## SHORT RESPONSE

*Cite Text Evidence* What information in the article and the diagram helps you understand how the trip was different for first-class passengers and steerage passengers of the *Titanic*? Be sure to **cite text evidence** from the diagram in your response.

# COLLECTION 4

# Making Your Voice Heard

COLLECTION 4

# Making Your Voice Heard

"When people don't express themselves, they die one piece at a time."

—Laurie Halse Anderson


INFORMATIONAL TEXTS

Views on Zoos

SHORT STORY

What Do Fish Have to Do with Anything? **Avi**

**Background** *The oldest known zoo existed in Hierakonpolis, Egypt, more than 5,500 years ago. It had hippos, elephants, baboons, and wildcats. In ancient times, a zoo was meant to display a leader's power and wealth. The purpose of today's zoos is different. For example, when the popular and vast Bronx Zoo opened in 1899, its purpose was to preserve native animals and promote zoology. Today, some people question whether zoos should exist at all.*

**CLOSE READ** Notes

1. **READ ▶** As you read lines 1–14, begin to collect and cite evidence.
   - Circle the main functions of a zoo.
   - Underline an example of each function (lines 3–14).
   - In the margin, summarize the functions of a zoo.

## Functions of a Zoo

Zoo **advocates** call attention to the main functions of a zoo: conservation, education and research, and recreation.

**advocates:**

- Animals that are constantly threatened in the wild are safe in a zoo, and they are well-fed and have medical care. Animals that are endangered can be bred in captivity, ensuring that their species do not die out.
- It is difficult to study animals in the wild; they are generally shy of humans and will avoid all contact. In the confines of a zoo enclosure, animal behavior can be studied. Animal responses to various conditions can be analyzed.
- Human beings have a natural curiosity about animals. Millions of people who otherwise could observe only a few animals in their lives can visit a zoo and marvel at the diversity of life on this planet.

# Sonia's Blog

## *Who I Am, What I Do—Every Day*

**Saturday, June 18**

The zoo! I visited the zoo with mom today. It's the same zoo she visited with her Mom. Mom said she remembers that the first thing you would see was a cage with two Siberian[1] tigers in it. But now the tigers have a new home, a huge area about the size of three football fields. They need it—they are huge themselves. One of the tigers weighs more than 600 pounds! They are my absolute favorite animals there. Go on the web and find some images of them, you'll understand.

We couldn't see everything in just one day, and luckily Mom and I both like the same animals. That means no snakes or insects! I always say I like all animals, so I'm a bit embarrassed to admit that I prefer the furry, cuddly ones (but when a tiger looks you in the eye, you know it isn't very cuddly).

There were elephants (cuddly?) and giraffes! Hippos! Monkeys of all kinds! I started wondering where they all came

[1] **Siberian:** from a region in northern Russia.

2. **REREAD** Reread lines 3–14 of "Functions of a Zoo." Restate the reasons zoo advocates cite in support of the existence of zoos.

3. **READ** As you read lines 1–41 of "Sonia's Blog," continue to cite evidence.
   - In the margin, state the topic of Sonia's blog entry.
   - Circle some positive statements Sonia makes about the zoo.
   - Underline some critical statements Sonia makes about the zoo.

from, and how they liked it here. I talked to some zookeepers. I guess it's obvious, but they all love animals, too. They take good care of them, and know each one's personality. But I couldn't help noticing a sad look in some of the animals' eyes. And they seemed defeated.

I can go jogging all around the pond and across the park, and then go with Mom to our friends way across town just to visit, that's what I can do. And then come home, and go to school the next day. Some of the animals had a faraway look that seemed to say how far they wanted to go, too. One of the keepers told me that a Siberian tiger (I know, I can't stop talking about those giant cats) can travel over 600 miles. Well, that's a long way away from the zoo.

So, I had a mixed experience. I loved seeing the animals, but I felt bad for some of them because they couldn't be themselves. I know, that's just me thinking I know what an animal would feel. But here's what I think: If you put me in a big apartment with everything I might need, it would be great. For a day or two. And then I would want to go and do the things I do every day and be myself. That's what this blog is all about.

What do you think about zoos? As usual, I want your comments.

4. **REREAD** Reread lines 1–10 of "Sonia's Blog". Explain how the zoo has changed over the years. Cite text evidence in your response.

accredits:

## Association of Zoos and Aquariums

The Association of Zoos and Aquariums (AZA) is an organization that **accredits** zoos, mostly in North America. This means that the AZA carefully makes sure that animals in zoos have suitable living environments, live together in their natural social groups, and are well taken care of, helping the animals to follow their natural behavior.

Most well-known zoos are members of the AZA, but of the animal exhibits in the United States, fewer than 10% are accredited. Worldwide, there are more than 10,000 zoos.

| AZA Statistics on Accredited Zoos | |
|---|---|
| Accredited Zoos and Aquariums | 221 |
| Animals | 752,000 |
| Species | 6,000 |
| Threatened or Endangered Species | 1,000 |
| Annual Visitors | 175 million |
| Annual Student Learners | 12 million |
| Jobs Supported | 142,000 |
| Annual Contribution to U.S. Economy | $16 billion |

5. **READ ▶** As you read lines 1–9 of "Association of Zoos and Aquariums" and study the chart, continue to cite text evidence.
   - Underline text that explains what the association is and the duties it carries out.
   - In the margin, summarize lines 7–9.
   - In the chart, circle the number of species housed in accredited zoos.

6. **◀ REREAD** Reread lines 1–9 and study the chart. What evidence could you cite that supports the existence of zoos?

# Innocent and Imprisoned

**Robert McGuinness** **July 22**

The elephant behind the fence is bobbing her head repeatedly, a sign of "zoochosis"—distress resulting from being in a zoo. In the wild, elephants roam about 30 miles each day in large groups. But not here, and one wonders what crime she could have committed to be behind bars. That's not the way it works, though. Violent and unpredictable animals are not the kind that are exhibited in zoos. The zoo inmates are all innocent.

Of course, zoo conditions for animals have improved **vastly.** Cramped cages and incorrect diets have been replaced with open spaces and well-researched care. But it is impossible to recreate the living environment of a dolphin or a polar bear. A forty-year-long study showed that polar bears—along with lions, tigers, and cheetahs—exhibit great evidence of stress in captivity.

**vastly:**

So why are these animals locked up? One answer to the question is conservation, but only a tiny number of zoos breed animals for conservation, and they release very few animals. During the twentieth century, there were 145 attempts to reintroduce populations into the wild, and only 16 of them were successful. The only way to **guarantee** a species' survival is to preserve them in the wild. Anyway, fewer than 15% of the animals on display are endangered. Many of the others are in zoos because of their **"charisma."** These are animals that paying customers want to see.

**guarantee:**

**charisma:**

There's another reason for keeping animals under lock and key: research. In some cases, this may be helpful to the animal populations as a whole, but to me it seems unscientific. Information gained from studying animals in unnatural situations is only reliable about animals in unnatural situations.

**7.** **READ ▶** As you read lines 1–45 of "Innocent and Imprisoned," cite text evidence.

- Underline evidence in lines 14–23 that opposes the existence of zoos.
- Circle the counterargument in lines 24–28. Underline evidence that addresses this counterargument.
- In the margin, restate the claim of the editorial in your own words.

Zoos also provide their customers an education. In most cases, however, the information given about an animal is very brief and presented on a small sign that few people bother to read. People tend to talk to their friends as they watch the exotic animals, rather than learn about their particular traits and characteristics. Visitors may watch in surprise as lions choose the freezing outdoors over heated shelters, but never learn that these animals once roamed freely throughout Europe.

The final main reason for having zoos is entertainment. This is obviously unfair to the animals that are imprisoned to entertain us. There are numerous television shows and movies that show us animals in their natural environments, behaving in ways that are natural to them.

A zoo that really suited animals would be a failure. It would be huge, and many of the animals would remain out of sight. The money spent supporting zoos would be better used trying to save animals in their natural surroundings, where they belong.

---

**8.** **REREAD AND DISCUSS** Reread lines 1–45. With a small group, discuss whether you find the writer's argument convincing. Cite reasons and evidence from the text that you find are the strongest or the weakest.

## SHORT RESPONSE

*Cite Text Evidence* What is your position on the existence of zoos? Write an argument in favor of or against zoos. **Cite text evidence** to support your claim and address any counterarguments.

**Background** **Avi** *says he became a writer out of sheer stubbornness. In elementary school and high school, he failed many subjects, not knowing that he suffered from a serious learning disability. Still, he was determined to prove that he could write if he set his mind to it. First, Avi wrote for adults with little success. He didn't discover his true audience until he became a father and took an interest in writing for children and young adults. He has written over 70 books and received the Newbury Medal and the Newbury Honor award for his work.*

# What Do Fish Have to Do with Anything?

Short Story by Avi

1. **READ ▶** As you read lines 1–23, begin to collect and cite text evidence.
   - Underline details that describe Willie's behavior.
   - In the margin, explain why Willie feels lonely.
   - Circle details that describe the man Willie sees (lines 17–23).

Every day at three o'clock Mrs. Markham waited for her son, Willie, to come out of school. They walked home together. If asked why she did it, Mrs. Markham would say, "Parents need to watch their children."

As they left the schoolyard, Mrs. Markham inevitably asked, "How was school?"

Willie would begin to talk, then stop. He was never sure his mother was listening. She seemed **preoccupied** with her own thoughts. She had been like that ever since his dad had abandoned them six months ago. No one knew where he'd gone. Willie had the feeling that his mother was lost too. It made him feel lonely.

**preoccupied:**

One Monday afternoon, as they approached the apartment building where they lived, she suddenly tugged at him. "Don't look that way," she said.

**CLOSE READ** Notes

"Where?"

"At that man over there."

Willie stole a look over his shoulder. A man, whom Willie had never seen before, was sitting on a red plastic milk crate near the curb. His matted, streaky gray hair hung like a ragged curtain over his dirty face. His shoes were torn. Rough hands lay upon his knees. One hand was palm up. No one seemed to pay him any mind. Willie was certain he had never seen a man so utterly alone. It was as if he were some spat-out piece of chewing gum on the pavement.

"What's the matter with him?" Willie asked his mother in a hushed voice.

Keeping her eyes straight ahead, Mrs. Markham said, "He's sick." She pulled Willie around. "Don't stare. It's rude."

"What kind of sick?"

As Mrs. Markham searched for an answer, she began to walk faster. "He's unhappy," she said.

"What's he doing?"

"Come on, Willie, you know perfectly well. He's begging."

"Do you think anyone gave him anything?"

"I don't know. Now, come on, don't look."

"Why don't you give him anything?"

"We have nothing to spare."

2. **REREAD** Reread lines 1–23. What does Willie's action in line 17 reveal about his character? Support your answer with text evidence.

3. **READ** As you read lines 24–61, continue to cite text evidence.

- Underline the questions that Willie asks his mother in lines 24–36.
- In the margin, restate in your own words the most significant thing Mrs. Markham says in lines 49–52.
- Circle what Mrs. Markham does that reminds Willie of the homeless man.



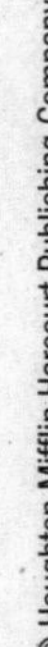

CLOSE READ
Notes

When they got home, Mrs. Markham removed a white cardboard box from the refrigerator. It contained pound cake. Using her thumb as a measure, she carefully cut a half-inch piece of cake and gave it to Willie on a clean plate. The plate lay on a plastic mat decorated with images of roses with diamondlike dewdrops. She also gave him a glass of milk and a folded napkin. She moved slowly.

Willie said, "Can I have a bigger piece of cake?"

Mrs. Markham picked up the cake box and ran a **manicured** pink fingernail along the nutrition information panel. "A half-inch piece is a portion, and a portion contains the following health requirements. Do you want to hear them?"

manicured:

"No."

"It's on the box, so you can believe what it says. Scientists study people, then write these things. If you're smart enough you could become a scientist. Like this." Mrs. Markham tapped the box. "It pays well."

Willie ate his cake and drank the milk. When he was done he took care to wipe the crumbs off his face as well as to blot his milk mustache with the napkin. His mother liked him to be neat.

His mother said, "Now go on and do your homework. Carefully. You're in sixth grade. It's important."

Willie gathered up his books that lay on the empty third chair. At the kitchen entrance he paused and looked back at his mother. She was staring sadly at the cake box, but he didn't think she was seeing it. Her unhappiness made him think of the man on the street.

**4.** **REREAD** Reread lines 37–52. What can you infer about Mrs. Markham based on her dialogue and the description of her behavior?

---

---

---

**5.** **READ** As you read lines 62–88, continue to cite text evidence.

- Underline each occurrence of the word *unhappiness.*
- Circle answers that Mrs. Markham gives that do not really address Willie's questions.
- In the margin, explain the salesman's quotation in line 81.

"What *kind* of unhappiness do you think he has?" he suddenly asked.

"Who's that?"

"That man."

Mrs. Markham looked puzzled.

"The begging man. The one on the street."

vaguely:

"Oh, could be anything," his mother said, **vaguely**,. "A person can be unhappy for many reasons." She turned to stare out the window, as if an answer might be there.

"Is unhappiness a sickness you can cure?"

"I wish you wouldn't ask such questions."

"Why?"

After a moment she said, "Questions that have no answers shouldn't be asked."

"Can I go out?"

"Homework first."

Willie turned to go again.

"Money," Mrs. Markham suddenly said. "Money will cure a lot of unhappiness. That's why that man was begging. A salesman once said to me, 'Maybe you can't buy happiness, but you can rent a lot of it.' You should remember that."

"How much money do we have?"

"Not enough."

"Is that why you're unhappy?"

"Willie, do your homework."

Willie started to ask another question, but decided he would not get an answer. He left the kitchen.

**6.** ◀ **REREAD AND DISCUSS** Reread lines 62–88. In a small group, discuss the reasons why Mrs. Markham avoids responding to Willie's questions about unhappiness.

**7.** **READ** ▶ As you read lines 89–134, continue to cite text evidence.

- Underline instances of Willie looking at the homeless man.
- In the margin, describe the way the dog and Willie are similar.
- Circle the text in which Willie disobeys his mother (lines 120–134).

The apartment had three rooms. The walls were painted mint green. Willie walked down the hallway to his room, which was at the front of the building. By climbing up on the windowsill and pressing against the glass he could see the sidewalk five stories below. The man was still there.

It was almost five when he went to tell his mother he had finished his school assignments. He found her in her dim bedroom, sleeping. Since she had begun working the night shift at a convenience store —two weeks now—she took naps in the late afternoon.

For a while Willie stood on the **threshold**, hoping his mother would wake up. When she didn't, he went to the front room and looked down on the street again. The begging man had not moved.

**threshold:**

Willie returned to his mother's room.

"I'm going out," he announced—softly.

Willie waited a decent interval for his mother to waken. When she did not, he made sure his keys were in his pocket. Then he left the apartment.

By standing just outside the building door, he could keep his eyes on the man. It appeared as if he had still not moved. Willie wondered how anyone could go without moving for so long in the chill October air. Was staying still part of the man's sickness?

During the twenty minutes that Willie watched, no one who passed looked in the beggar's direction. Willie wondered if they even saw the man. Certainly no one put any money into his open hand.

A lady leading a dog by a leash went by. The dog strained in the direction of the man sitting on the crate. His tail wagged. The lady pulled the dog away. "Heel!" she commanded.

The dog—tail between his legs—scampered to the lady's side. Even so, the dog twisted around to look back at the beggar.

Willie grinned. The dog had done exactly what Willie had done when his mother told him not to stare.

Pressing deep into his pocket, Willie found a nickel. It was warm and slippery. He wondered how much happiness you could rent for a nickel.

Squeezing the nickel between his fingers, Willie walked slowly toward the man. When he came before him, he stopped, suddenly nervous. The man, who appeared to be looking at the ground, did not move his eyes. He smelled bad.

"Here." Willie stretched forward and dropped the coin into the man's open right hand.

"God bless you," the man said hoarsely as he folded his fingers over the coin. His eyes, like high beams on a car, flashed up at Willie, then dropped.

Willie waited for a moment, then went back up to his room. From his window he looked down on the street. He thought he saw the coin in the man's hand, but was not sure.

After supper Mrs. Markham readied herself to go to work, then kissed Willie good night. As she did every night, she said, "If you have regular problems, call Mrs. Murphy downstairs. What's her number?"

"274-8676," Willie said.

"Extra bad problems, call Grandma."

"369-6754."

"Super special problems, you can call me."

"962-6743."

"Emergency, the police."

"911."

"Lay out your morning clothing."

"I will."

"Don't let anyone in the door."

"I won't."

"No television past nine."

"I know."

"But you can read late."

**8.** **◀ REREAD** Reread lines 120–134. Why does Willie give money to the homeless man, especially since his mother told him to stay away?

**9.** **READ ▶** As you read lines 135–164, continue to cite text evidence.

- In the margin, explain why Willie has all these phone numbers.
- Underline what Willie learns about the fish that live in caves.
- Circle the teacher's responses to Willie's questions.

"You're the one who's going to be late," Willie reminded her.

"I'm leaving," Mrs. Markham said.

After she went, Willie stood for a long while in the hallway. The empty apartment felt like a cave that lay deep below the earth. That day in school Willie's teacher had told the class about a kind of fish that lived in caves. These fish could not see. They had no eyes. The teacher had said it was living in the dark cave that made them like that.

Willie had raised his hand and asked, "If they want to get out of the cave, can they?"

"I suppose."

"Would their eyes come back?"

"Good question." she said, but did not give an answer.

Before he went to bed, Willie took another look out the window. In the pool of light cast by the street lamp, Willie saw the man.

On Tuesday morning when Willie went to school, the man was gone. But when he came home from school with his mother, he was there again.

"*Please* don't look at him," his mother whispered with some urgency.

During his snack, Willie said, "Why shouldn't I look?"

"What are you talking about?"

"That man. On the street. Begging."

"I told you. He's sick. It's better to act as if you never saw him. When people are that way they don't wish to be looked at."

**10.** **REREAD** Reread lines 154–164. What does the dialogue between Willie and his teacher reveal about Willie's character?

**11.** **READ** As you read lines 165–217, continue to cite text evidence.

- Underline details that show Willie's father was unhappy.
- In the margin, make an inference about why Willie's mother wishes Willie would not ask about her being unhappy.
- Circle the moment in the conversation when Willie mentions the sightless fish.

"Why not?"

Mrs. Markham pondered for a while. "People are ashamed of being unhappy."

Willie looked thoughtfully at his mother. "Are you sure he's unhappy?"

"You don't have to ask if people are unhappy. They tell you all the time."

"How?"

"The way they look."

"Is that part of the sickness?"

"Oh, Willie, I don't know. It's just the way they are."

contemplate:

Willie **contemplated** the half-inch slice of cake his mother had just given him. A year ago his parents seemed to be perfectly happy. For Willie, the world seemed easy, full of light. Then his father lost his job. He tried to get another but could not. For long hours he sat in dark rooms. Sometimes he drank. His parents began to argue a lot. One day, his father was gone.

For two weeks his mother kept to the dark. And wept.

Willie looked at his mother. "You're unhappy," he said. "Are *you* ashamed?"

Mrs. Markham sighed and closed her eyes. "I wish you wouldn't ask that."

"Why?"

"It hurts me."

"But are you ashamed?" Willie persisted. He felt it was urgent that he know. So that he could do something.

She only shook her head.

Willie said, "Do you think Dad might come back?"

She hesitated before saying, "Yes, I think so."

Willie wondered if that was what she really thought.

"Do you think Dad is unhappy?" Willie asked.

"Where do you get such questions?"

"They're in my mind."

"There's much in the mind that need not be paid attention to."

"Fish who live in caves have no eyes."

"What are you talking about?"

"My teacher said it's all that darkness. The fish forget how to see. So they lose their eyes."

"I doubt she said that."

"She did."

"Willie, you have too much imagination."

After his mother went to work, Willie gazed down onto the street. The man was there. Willie thought of going down, but he knew he was not supposed to leave the building when his mother worked at night. He decided to speak to the man the next day.

That afternoon—Wednesday—Willie stood before the man. "I don't have any money," Willie said. "Can I still talk to you?"

The man lifted his face. It was a dirty face with very tired eyes. He needed a shave.

"My mother," Willie began, "said you were unhappy. Is that true?"

"Could be," the man said.

"What are you unhappy about?"

The man's eyes narrowed as he studied Willie **intently.** He said, "How come you want to know?"

**intently:**

Willie shrugged.

"I think you should go home, kid."

"I am home." Willie gestured toward the apartment. "I live right here. Fifth floor. Where do you live?"

"Around."

"*Are* you unhappy?" Willie persisted.

The man ran a tongue over his lips. His Adam's apple bobbed. "A man has the right to remain silent," he said, and closed his eyes.

**12.** **REREAD** Reread lines 195–217. Why does Willie bring up the sightless fish during their conversation?

**13.** **READ** As you read lines 218–264, continue to cite text evidence.

- Underline text that describes the man's appearance and behavior.
- Circle what the homeless man says to Willie in lines 237–247.
- In the margin, explain why Willie wants to find the cure for unhappiness.

Willie remained standing on the pavement for a while before retreating back to his apartment. Once inside he looked down from the window. The man was still there. For a moment Willie was certain the man was looking at the apartment building and the floor where Willie lived.

The next day, Thursday—after dropping a nickel in the man's palm—Willie said, "I've never seen anyone look so unhappy as you do. So I figure you must know a lot about it."

The man took a deep breath. "Well, yeah, maybe."

Willie said, "And I need to find a cure for it."

"A *what*?"

"A cure for unhappiness."

The man pursed his cracked lips and blew a silent whistle. Then he said, "Why?"

"My mother is unhappy."

"Why's that?"

"My dad went away."

"How come?"

"I think because he was unhappy. Now my mother's unhappy too—all the time. So if I found a cure for unhappiness, it would be a good thing, wouldn't it?"

"I suppose. Hey, you don't have anything to eat on you, do you?"

Willie shook his head, then said, "Would you like some cake?"

"What kind?"

"I don't know. Cake."

**14.** **REREAD** Reread lines 218–264. What does the homeless man's dialogue and behavior suggest about his character?

**15.** **READ** As you read lines 265–297, continue to cite text evidence.

- Underline the reasons why the homeless man believes Willie.
- Circle Willie's "grown-up name."
- In the margin, note differences between Willie's discussion with the man in lines 270–283 and his conversation with his mother in lines 211–217.

"Depends on the cake."

On Friday Willie said to the man, "I found out what kind of cake it is."

"Yeah?"

"Pound cake. But I don't know why it's called that."

"Long as it's cake it probably don't matter."

Neither spoke. Then Willie said, "In school my teacher said there are fish who live in caves and the caves are so dark the fish don't have eyes. What do you think? Do you believe that?"

"Sure."

"You do? How come?"

"Because you said so."

"You mean, just because someone *said* it you believe it?"

"Not someone. You."

Willie was puzzled. "But, well, maybe it *isn't* true."

The man grunted. "Hey, do you believe it?"

Willie nodded.

"Well, you're not just anyone. You got eyes. You see. You ain't no fish."

"Oh." Willie was pleased.

"What's your name?" the man asked.

"Willie."

"That's a boy's name. What's your grown-up name?"

"William."

"And that means another thing."

"What?"

"I'll take some of that cake."

Willie started. "You will?" he asked, surprised.

"Just said it, didn't I?"

Willie suddenly felt excited. It was as if the man had given him a gift. Willie wasn't sure what it was except that it was important and he was glad to have it. For a moment he just gazed at the man. He saw the lines on the man's face, the way his lips curved, the small scar on the side of his chin, the shape of his eyes, which he now saw were blue.

**16.** **REREAD AND DISCUSS** Reread lines 270–283. In a small group, discuss why the homeless man says Willie's "got eyes." Cite evidence from the text to support your interpretation.

"I'll get the cake," Willie cried and ran back to the apartment. He snatched the box from the refrigerator as well as a knife, then hurried back down to the street. "I'll cut you a piece," he said, and he opened the box.

"Hey, that don't look like a pound of cake," the man said.

Willie, alarmed, looked up.

"But like I told you, it don't matter."

Willie held his thumb against the cake to make sure the portion was the right size. With a poke of the knife he made a small mark for the proper width.

Just as he was about to cut, the man said, "Hold it!"

Willie looked up. "What?"

"What were you doing there with your thumb?"

"I was measuring the size. The right portion. A person is supposed to get only one portion."

"Where'd you learn that?"

"It says so on the box. You can see for yourself." He held out the box.

The man studied the box then handed it back to Willie. "That's just lies," he said.

"How do you know?"

"William, how can a box say how much a person needs?"

"But it does. The scientists say so. They measured, so they know. Then they put it there."

"Lies," the man repeated.

Willie began to feel that this man knew many things. "Well, then, how much should I cut?" he asked.

The man said, "You have to look at me, then at the cake, and then you're going to have to decide for yourself."

"Oh." Willie looked at the cake. The piece was about three inches wide. Willie looked up at the man. After a moment he cut the cake into two pieces, each an inch and a half wide. He gave one piece to the man and kept the other in the box.

**17.** READ ▶ As you read lines 298–349, continue to cite text evidence.

- In the margin, explain why Willie measures the cake the way he does.
- Circle the man's advice to Willie on the amount of cake to cut.
- Underline the man's "cure for unhappiness." In the margin, explain what he means.

"God bless you," the man said as he took the piece and laid it in his left hand. He began to break off pieces with his right hand and put them in his mouth one by one. Each piece was chewed thoughtfully. Willie watched him eat.

When the man was done, he licked the crumbs on his fingers.

"Now I'll give you something," the man said.

"What?" Willie said, surprised.

"The cure for unhappiness."

"You know it?" Willie asked, eyes wide.

The man nodded.

"What is it?"

"It's this: What a person needs is always more than they say."

"Who's *they?*" Willie asked.

The man pointed to the cake box. "The people on the box," he said.

In his mind Willie repeated what he had been told, then he gave the man the second piece of cake.

The man took it, saying, "Good man," and he ate it.

Willie grinned.

**18.** **◀ REREAD** Reread lines 305–349. Why does Willie give the man all of the cake? In what ways does his decision indicate that he has changed as a person?

The next day was Saturday. Willie did not go to school. All morning he kept looking down from his window for the man, but it was raining and he did not appear. Willie wondered where he was, but could not imagine it.

Willie's mother woke about noon. Willie sat with her while she ate her breakfast. "I found the cure for unhappiness," he announced.

"Did you?" his mother said. She was reading a memo from the convenience store's owner.

"It's 'What a person needs is always more than they say.'"

His mother put her papers down. "That's nonsense. Where did you hear that?"

"That man."

"What man?"

"On the street. The one who was begging. You said he was unhappy. So I asked him."

"Willie, I told you I didn't want you to even look at that man."

"He's a nice man. . . ."

"How do you know?"

"I've talked to him."

"When? How much?"

Willie shrank down. "I did, that's all."

"Willie, I forbid you to talk to him. Do you understand me? Do you? Answer me!" She was shrill.

"Yes," Willie said, but he'd already decided he would talk to the man one more time. He needed to explain why he could not talk to him anymore.

**19.** **READ ▶** As you read lines 350–375, continue to cite text evidence.

- Underline Willie's mother's reaction to the cure for unhappiness.
- Circle the text that tells you Willie's mother is angry with him.
- In the margin, restate the reason why Willie is going to speak to the man again.

**20.** **◀ REREAD** Reread lines 365–375. Why is Willie's mother so upset with him? What is Willie's reaction to her anger?

______________________________

______________________________

______________________________

> **"What a person needs is always more than they say."**

On Sunday, however, the man was not there. Nor was he there on Monday.

"That man is gone," Willie said to his mother as they walked home from school.

"I saw. I'm not blind."

"Where do you think he went?"

"I couldn't care less. But you might as well know, I arranged for him to be gone."

Willie stopped short. "What do you mean?"

"I called the police. We don't need a nuisance like that around here. Pestering kids."

"He wasn't pestering me."

"Of course he was."

"How do you know?"

"Willie, I have eyes. I can see."

Willie glared at his mother. "No, you can't. You're a fish. You live in a cave."

**21.** **READ ▶** As you read lines 376–400, continue to cite text evidence.

- Underline details in lines 376–386 that explain what has happened to the homeless man.
- Circle the dialogue that refers to the sightless fish.
- In the margin, explain why Willie insists on being called William.

"Fish?" retorted Mrs. Markham. "What do fish have to do with anything? Willie, don't talk nonsense."

"My name isn't Willie. It's William. And I know how to keep from being unhappy. I do!" He was yelling now. "What a person needs is always more than they say! *Always*!"

He turned on his heel and walked back toward the school. At the corner he glanced back. His mother was following. He kept going. She kept following.

**22.** **REREAD** Reread lines 376–400. What does the sightless fish represent to Willie? Why does he call his mother a fish? Cite explicit textual evidence in your answer.

## SHORT ANSWER

*Cite Text Evidence* How does Willie grow and change as the story progresses? Review the notes you took as you read and **cite text evidence** in your response.

COLLECTION **5**

# Decisions That Matter

COLLECTION 5

# Decisions That Matter

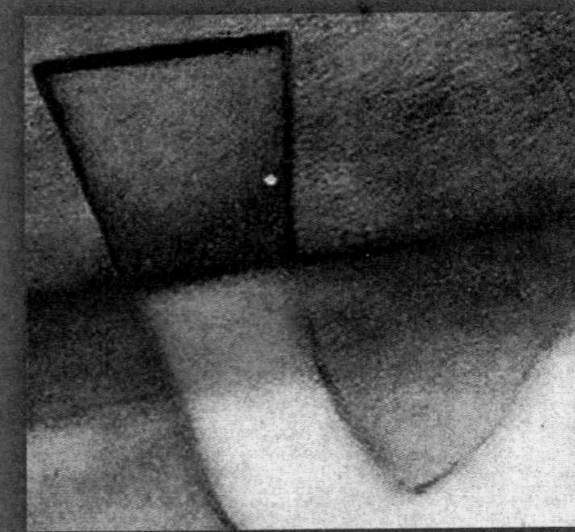

"We must never forget that it is through our actions, words, and thoughts that we have a choice."

—Sogyal Rinpoche


BIOGRAPHY

Community Hero: Chief Wilma Mankiller — **Susannah Abbey**

AUTOBIOGRAPHY

*from* Every Day Is a New Day — **Wilma Mankiller**

POEM

The Light—Ah! The Light — **Joyce Sidman**

**Background** Wilma Mankiller *(1945–2010) was born in Oklahoma, the sixth of 11 children. She grew up in a home without electricity, indoor plumbing, or a telephone. In the 1950s, the Mankiller family was relocated by the Bureau of Indian Affairs and moved to San Francisco. Mankiller was the first woman to be elected principal chief of the Cherokee Nation. As chief, she worked to improve the nation's health care, government, and education system. She continued to be an active presence in the Cherokee Nation after she left office and was particularly dedicated to working for women's rights.*

# Community Hero: Chief Wilma Mankiller

By Susannah Abbey

# *from* Every Day Is a New Day

By Wilma Mankiller

1. **READ ▶** As you read lines 1–31 of "Community Hero," begin to collect and cite text evidence.
   - Underline facts about Wilma Mankiller's childhood.
   - Circle the role the San Francisco Indian Center played in Mankiller's life.

## Community Hero: Chief Wilma Mankiller

Biography by Susannah Abbey

Wilma Mankiller came from a large family that spent many years on the family farm in Oklahoma. They were, of course, poor, but not desperately so. "As far back as I can remember there were always books around our house," she recalls in her autobiography, *Mankiller: A Chief and Her People.* "This love of reading came from the traditional Cherokee passion for telling and listening to stories. But it also came from my parents, particularly my father . . . A love for books and reading was one of the best gifts he ever gave his children."

Unfortunately, a poor local economy made the Mankiller family an easy target for the Bureau of Indian Affairs relocation program of the 1950s. Government agents were entrusted with the job of moving rural Cherokees to cities, effectively dispersing them and allowing others to buy their traditional, oil-rich lands. In 1959 the family moved to San Francisco, where Wilma's father could get a job and where Wilma began her junior high school years. This was not a happy time for her. She missed the farm and she hated the school where white kids teased her about being Native American and about her name.

Mankiller decided to leave her parents and go to live with her maternal grandmother, Pearl Sitton, on a family ranch inland from San Francisco. The year she spent there restored her confidence and after returning to the Bay Area, she got increasingly involved with the world of the San Francisco Indian Center.

"There was something at the Center for everyone. It was a safe place to go, even if we only wanted to hang out." The Center provided entertainment, social and cultural activities for youth, as well as a place for adults to hold powwows and discuss matters of importance with other BIA relocatees. Here, Mankiller became politicized, at the same time reinforcing her identity as a Cherokee and her attachments to the Cherokee people, their history and traditions.

**2.** **◀ REREAD** Reread lines 10–31. In the margin, list three important events in Mankiller's life. Why does the author include information about Mankiller's childhood? Support your answer with explicit textual evidence.

______________________________________________

______________________________________________

______________________________________________

**3.** **READ ▶** As you read lines 32–79, continue to cite textual evidence.

- Circle Mankiller's first political involvement.
- In the margin, explain why the Native American Youth Center was important to Mankiller's development as a leader. Circle an example to support your answer.
- Underline problems Mankiller encountered during her campaign.

**"Mankiller says she learned on the job. . . . But she was, in truth, a natural leader."**

When a group of Native Americans occupied Alcatraz Island in November 1969, in protest of U.S. Government policies, which had, for hundreds of years, deprived them of their lands, Mankiller participated in her first major political action.

"It changed me forever," she wrote. "It was on Alcatraz . . . where at long last some Native Americans, including me, truly began to regain our balance."

In the years that followed the "occupation," Mankiller became more active in developing the cultural resources of the Native American community. She helped build a school and an Indian Adult Education Center. She directed the Native American Youth Center in East Oakland, coordinating field trips to tribal functions, hosting music concerts, and giving kids a place to do their homework or just connect with each other. The youth center also gave her the opportunity to pull together Native American adults from around Oakland as volunteers, thus strengthening their ties. Mankiller says she learned on the job, joking "my enthusiasm seemed to make up for my lack of skills." But she was, in truth, a natural leader.

She returned to Oklahoma in the 1970s where she worked at the Urban Indian Resource Center and volunteered in the community. In 1981 she founded and then became director of the Cherokee Community Development Department, where she orchestrated a community-based **renovation** of the water system and was instrumental in lifting an entire town, Bell, Oklahoma, out of squalor and despair. In 1983, she ran for Deputy Chief of the Cherokee Nation.

**renovation:**

vindicate:

obligate:

The campaign was not an easy one. There had never been a woman leader of a Native American tribe. She had many ideas to present and debate, but encountered discouraging opposition from men who refused to talk about anything but the fact that she was a woman. Her campaign days were troubled by death threats, and her tires were slashed. She sought the advice of friends for ways to approach the constant insults, finally settling on a philosophy summed up by the epithet, "Don't ever argue with a fool, because someone walking by and observing you can't tell which one is the fool." In the end, Mankiller had her day: she was elected as first woman Deputy Chief, and over time her wise, strong leadership **vindicated** her supporters and proved her detractors wrong.

In 1985, when Chief Ross Swimmer left for Washington, D.C., Mankiller was **obligated** to step into his position, becoming the first woman to serve as Principal Chief of the Cherokee Nation. Although poor health forced her to retire from that position in 1995, Wilma Mankiller continues to be a political, cultural, and spiritual leader in her community and throughout the United States. In 1990 Oklahoma State University honored her with the Henry G. Bennett Distinguished Service Award, and in 1998, President Clinton awarded her the Presidential Medal of Freedom, the nation's highest civilian honor.

4. **REREAD AND DISCUSS** Reread lines 58–69. In a small group, discuss the possible reasons that men may have opposed having a woman as Chief. What experiences qualified Mankiller for the job? Be sure to cite evidence from the text in your discussion.

5. **READ ▶** As you read lines 1–41 from "Every Day Is a New Day," begin to collect and cite text evidence.

- In the margin, make an inference about how Mankiller feels about her surroundings, and underline descriptive language that supports your inference.
- In the margin, summarize the indigenous people's historical connection to Alcatraz.

## *from* Every Day Is a New Day
### Autobiography by Wilma Mankiller

Though I have lived most of my life on my grandfather's Cherokee land allotment in rural Adair County, Oklahoma, I learned a great deal about **indigenous** people, governance, and land during the twenty years I spent in the San Francisco Bay Area. Soon after my Native American brothers and sisters joined the occupation of Alcatraz Island in late 1969, I made plans to visit the island. The morning I made the short journey to Alcatraz, my heart and mind made a quantum leap forward.

**indigenous:**

Lady dawn descended on the nearly empty streets of Fisherman's Wharf, bearing the gift of a brand-new day. Fishing boasts rocked in their slips, awaiting the day's journey, as shop owners sleepily prepared for the onslaught of tourists. An occasional foghorn or the barking of a stray dog was the only sound other than the steady lap of the ocean against the docks. Alcatraz Island, several miles across San Francisco Bay, was barely visible as I boarded a boat for the former military and federal prison, which had recently been taken over by indigenous people and declared "Indian Land." Mist and fog gave the island a dreamlike quality that seemed fitting for a place where the American dream was rejected and an Indigenous dream declared.

The young students who occupied Alcatraz Island claimed that federal surplus lands such as Alcatraz should be returned to tribal peoples on legal and moral ground, and that treaties, land rights, and tribal **sovereignty** should be respected and honored. This was not the first relationship between indigenous people and Alcatraz. Long before Europeans arrived, Ohlones and other indigenous people of

**sovereignty:**

Alcatraz Island

the coast rested and got their bearings on Alcatraz Island, called the Island of the Pelicans (Isla de los Alcatraces) after the seabirds that gathered there. In the late nineteenth century, Modocs and other tribal people were imprisoned at Alcatraz for fighting the United States Army in a desperate attempt to retain their ancestral homelands. When the Spanish first settled in the mid-1700s on the land that is today California, there were more than 275,000 indigenous people living there. That changed very quickly. By 1900, fewer than 16,000 indigenous people remained. It is a miracle that even that many survived. Indigenous people of California endured widespread violence, starvation, disease, genocide, rape, and slavery. As late as 1870, a few communities in California were still paying bounties for Indian scalps or severed heads. One hundred years later, the descendants of some of the indigenous people who survived the conquerors, miners, and settlers joined others at Alcatraz to find their bearings just as their ancestors had done so long ago.

6. **REREAD AND DISCUSS** Reread lines 20–41. In a small group, explain why Alcatraz Island holds such importance for Mankiller.

7. **READ** As you read lines 42–87, continue to cite textual evidence.
   - Underline sentences that explain what Alcatraz symbolized for younger American Indians.
   - Circle two pieces of information that Mankiller learns about sovereignty.

I visited Alcatraz several times during the nineteen-month occupation of the island. At any given time, the Alcatraz community was composed of an **eclectic** group of indigenous people, activists, civil rights veterans, students, and people who just wanted to be at a "happening." Richard Oakes, a visionary young Mohawk who emerged as an early spokesman for the Alcatraz occupiers, said, "There are many old prophecies that speak of the younger people rising up and finding a way for the People to live." (In their own languages, many tribes call themselves by words that mean "the People.") Alcatraz was a catalyst for many young people who would spend their lives forging a new path for the People.

**eclectic:**

The Alcatraz experience was certainly a **watershed** for me. The leaders articulated principles and ideas I had thought about but could not name or articulate. During the Alcatraz occupation and that period of activism, anything seemed possible. Inspired by Alcatraz, I began a four-year association with the Pit River Tribe, which was involved in a legal and political struggle to regain their ancestral lands near Mount Shasta. Mostly I worked as a volunteer at the tribe's legal offices in San Francisco, but I frequently visited Pit River lands, where I learned about the history of indigenous people in California from traditional leaders. Occasionally one of the leaders would bring out an old cardboard box filled with tribal documents supporting their land claims. They treated the precious documents almost as sacred objects. At Pit River, I learned that sovereignty was more than a legal concept. It represents the ability of the People to articulate their own vision of the future, control their destiny, and watch over their lands. It means freedom and responsibility.

**watershed:**

Another place that had a great impact on me was the Oakland Intertribal Friendship House, which served as an oasis for a diverse group of indigenous people living in a busy urban area far from their home communities. We gathered there for dinners, meetings, and to listen to a wonderful array of speakers, including Tom Porter, a Mohawk leader who spoke about his people's fight to remain separate

and independent. He explained that the Mohawk's 1795 treaty with the United States provided that they had the "perpetual right to live on their reservations in independent sovereignty, never to be disturbed." He spoke movingly about the important role women play among his people. He said that traditional Iroquois women selected the chiefs and could **depose** them if they did not perform their duties properly. The speech had a powerful, lasting impact on me.

depose:

My experiences at Alcatraz and Pit River led me to cofound, with Joe Carillo, California Indians for a Fair Settlement, which encouraged California tribal people to reject a proposed settlement of all land claims for only pennies per acre. All this work helped me to understand more fully the historical context in which tribal people live our contemporary lives.

galvanize:

In 1976 I was further **galvanized** by a treaty conference at the Standing Rock Sioux Reservation in Wakpala, South Dakota, that readied delegates for the 1977 United Nations Conference on

**8.** **◀ REREAD** Reread lines 53–87. Summarize what Mankiller learns from her work at Alcatraz, with the Pit River Tribe, and in Oakland. What did her experiences teach her? Support your answer with explicit textual evidence.

**9.** **READ ▶** As you read lines 88–116, continue to cite textual evidence.

- Underline the relationship between political and spiritual organizations in the present and in the past.
- Circle what Mankiller thought of her experiences with the tribes.

> **"All peoples have the right to self-determination."**

Indigenous Rights in Geneva. I had been working as a volunteer to help indigenous people prepare for the Geneva conference by documenting the fact that from the time of initial contact with Europeans, tribal communities were treated as separate nations, and numerous agreements between the emerging United States and tribal nations were signed.

At Wakpala, tribal sovereignty was framed as an issue of international significance. The concept of self-determination in international law as defined by UN General Assembly Resolution 1514 resonates with indigenous people: "All peoples have the right to self-determination. By virtue of that right they freely determine their political status and freely pursue their economic, social, and cultural development."

During this time, I also came to understand that among some tribal people, including the Cherokee, there was a historical period when there was little separation between political and spiritual organizations. Cherokee spiritual leaders were involved in conducting the council meetings that provided some of the political structure whereby major decisions were made by the entire settlement. Council meetings were often held after or during ceremonies, which helped prepare the people to deal with major issues affecting the community. However, in contemporary times, there is a formal separation between the political organization and spiritual practitioners.

The Alcatraz, Pit River, California Indian for a Fair Settlement, and the treaty Conference experiences were great preparation for my future role as principal chief of the Cherokee Nation.

**10.** **◀ REREAD AND DISCUSS** Reread lines 97–103. Work with a small group to paraphrase the concept of self-determination as stated by UN General Assembly Resolution 1514. Why did this resolution mean so much to Mankiller? Cite explicit text evidence in your discussion.

## SHORT RESPONSE

*Cite Text Evidence* In what ways is Wilma Mankiller's autobiographical account of her life different from Susannah Abbey's biography? Compare and contrast the information presented in each text. Review your reading notes for both texts, and be sure to **cite text evidence** in your response.

**Background** *Born in 1956,* **Joyce Sidman** *is an award-winning American writer known for her inventive poetry. Her poem, "The Light—Ah! The Light" takes as its subject the physicist and chemist Marie Curie. Born Marie Skłodowska in Warsaw, Poland, in 1867, Marie Curie studied at the University of Paris (referred in the poem as the Sorbonne) and discovered the chemical elements polonium and radium. She is best known for discovering the principles of radioactivity, which refers to the loss of particles and energy from certain atomic elements. Sidman reimagines Curie's thoughts and feelings in the poem.*

# The Light—Ah! The Light

## (Marie Curie discovered the principles of radioactivity.)

Poem by Joyce Sidman

**CLOSE READ** Notes

1. **READ ▶** As you read lines 1–34, begin to cite text evidence.
   - Underline words and phrases in lines 1–6 that reveal the setting.
   - In the margin, explain what happens in the last three stanzas.
   - Underline details that describe the effect that working with radioactive materials has on Curie.

First of all, I am a Pole.
Manya, they called me
when I was a girl in Warsaw,
under the dark **yoke** of Russian rule.
We hid our Polish grammars
and spit at the obelisk erected by the Tsar.

But I was drawn to Paris
as a plant is drawn to the light.
And the Sorbonne, despite its
pointed little men,
shone like the sun itself.
Poverty, prejudice, the infuriating
French language—all this,
like a handful of cobwebs,
I swept aside.

**yoke:**

incinerate:

For the subject of my doctorate,
I chose uranium.
Just a lump of stone—but it shone!
The work was brutal:
a ton of ore to be hauled, cracked, **incinerated**
for one pure gram of radium.
I kept a bowl of it at my bedside
so I could wake at night
to its fairy glow.

In the end,
that glow ravaged my skin,
poisoned my blood.
I was like the shell of a burned-out tree.
But what of it?
I, Manya,
the poor Polish girl from Warsaw,
pried open life's hidden heart
and discovered the bright burn
of its decay.

2. **REREAD AND DISCUSS** Reread lines 1–34. With a small group, discuss details from the poem that convey Curie's pride in her achievements.

## SHORT RESPONSE

*Cite Text Evidence* What do you learn about Marie Curie from the way she responds to her circumstances? Review your reading notes and **cite text evidence** in your response.

COLLECTION 6

# What Tales Tell

COLLECTION **6**

# What Tales Tell

"The destiny of the world is determined less by the battles that are lost and won than by the stories it loves and believes in."

—Harold Goddard


**GREEK MYTH**

Medusa's Head — ***retold by*** **Olivia E. Coolidge**

**POEM**

Medusa — **Agha Shahid Ali**

**Comparing Versions of The Prince and the Pauper**

**NOVEL**

*from* The Prince and the Pauper — **Mark Twain**

**DRAMA**

*from* The Prince and the Pauper — **Mark Twain**
***dramatized by*** **Joellen Bland**

**GRAPHIC STORY**

*from* The Prince and the Pauper — **Marvel Comics**

**Background** *According to Greek myth, Medusa was one of three beautiful sisters known as the Gorgons. The sisters were turned into monsters by Athene, the goddess of wisdom, who was angry at the destruction of one of her temples. Medusa was turned into a horrific creature with a gaping mouth, hypnotic eyes, and hair made of writhing snakes. Anyone who looked into Medusa's eyes was immediately turned to stone.*

# Medusa's Head

Retold by Olivia E. Coolidge

# Medusa

By Agha Shahid Ali

**Olivia E. Coolidge** *(1909–2006) was enjoying a perfectly normal childhood in London with a perfectly normal dislike for Greek literature when she twisted her ankle. For three months a cruel sprain kept her from going outside to play, so she read—and read. Soon she was reading Greek poetry and she made a shocking discovery: she loved it! Coolidge went on to write numerous books of Greek myths for young adults.*

**Agha Shahid Ali** *(1949–2001) was born in New Delhi, India, but he lived, studied, and taught in the United States for more than twenty-five years. Ali was a Kashmiri Muslim, but he identified himself as an American poet. Ali's poetry embraces multiple heritages (Hindu, Muslim, and Western) and crosses literary traditions. A joyful, brilliant poet, a man blessed with friends and honors, Ali died from a brain tumor at the age of 52.*

1. **READ ▶** As you read lines 1–37, begin to collect and cite text evidence.

- Circle what the oracle tells Acrisios.
- Summarize in the margin what Acrisios does to Danae.
- Underline the ways the gods help Danae.
- In the margin, explain Danae's behavior in lines 28–37.

## Medusa's Head

### Greek Myth retold by Olivia E. Coolidge

King Acrisios of Argos was a hard, selfish man. He hated his brother, Proitos, who later drove him from his kingdom and he cared nothing for his daughter, Danae. His whole heart was set on having a son who should succeed him, but since many years went by and still he had only the one daughter, he sent a message to the oracle of Apollo to ask whether he should have more children of his own. The answer of the oracle was terrible. Acrisios should have no son, but his daughter, Danae, would bear him a grandchild who should grow up to kill him. At these words Acrisios was beside himself with fear and rage. Swearing that Danae should never have a child to murder him, he had a room built underground and lined all through with brass. Thither he conducted Danae and shut her up, bidding her spend the rest of her life alone.

descend:

It is possible to thwart the plans of mortal men, but never those of the gods. Zeus himself looked with pity at the unfortunate girl, and it is said he **descended** to her through the tiny hole that gave light and air to her chamber, pouring himself down into her lap in the form of a shower of gold.

When word came to the king from those who brought food and drink to his daughter that the girl was with child, Acrisios was angry and afraid. He would have liked best to murder both Danae and her infant son, but he did not dare for fear of the gods' anger at so hideous a crime. He made, therefore, a great chest of wood with bands of brass about it. Shutting up the girl and her baby inside, he cast them into the sea, thinking that they would either drown or starve.

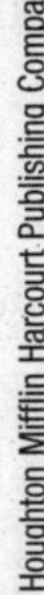

Again the gods came to the help of Danae, for they caused the planks of the chest to swell until they fitted tightly and let no water in.

The chest floated for some days and was cast up at last on an island. There Dictys, a fisherman, found it and took Danae to his brother, Polydectes, who was king of the island. Danae was made a servant in the palace, yet before many years had passed, both Dictys and Polydectes had fallen in love with the silent, golden-haired girl. She in her heart preferred Dictys, yet since his brother was king, she did not dare to make her choice. Therefore she hung always over Perseus, pretending that mother love left her no room for any other, and year after year a silent frown would cross Polydectes' face as he saw her caress the child.

At last, Perseus became a young man, handsome and strong beyond the common and a leader among the youths of the island, though he was but the son of a poor servant. Then it seemed to Polydectes that if he could once get rid of Perseus, he could force Danae to become his wife, whether she would or not. Meanwhile, in order to lull the young man's suspicions, he pretended that he intended to marry a certain noble maiden and would collect a wedding gift for her. Now the custom was that this gift of the

2. **REREAD** Reread lines 14–27. In what ways are the gods similar to humans? What superhuman powers do they have? Cite textual evidence in your response.

3. **READ** As you read lines 38–81, continue to cite textual evidence.

- In lines 38–52, circle Perseus's qualities that suggest he may be a hero.
- In the margin, explain why Polydectes feels "satisfaction" (line 66).
- Underline the items Perseus will use on his journey. In the margin, summarize the steps Perseus must take to slay the Gorgon.

bridegroom to the bride was in part his own and in part put together from the marriage presents of his friends and relatives. All the young men, therefore, brought Polydectes a present, excepting Perseus, who was his servant's son and possessed nothing to bring. Then Polydectes said to the others, "This young man owes me more than any of you, since I took him in and brought him up in my own house, and yet he gives me nothing."

Perseus answered in anger at the injustice of the charge, "I have nothing of my own, Polydectes, yet ask me what you will, and I will fetch it, for I owe you my life."

At this Polydectes smiled, for it was what he had intended, and he answered, "Fetch me, if this is your boast, the Gorgon's head."

Now the Gorgons, who lived far off on the shores of the ocean, were three fearful sisters with hands of brass, wings of gold, and scales like a serpent. Two of them had scaly heads and tusks like the wild boar, but the third, Medusa, had the face of a beautiful woman with hair of writhing serpents, and so terrible was her expression that all who looked on it were immediately turned to stone. This much Perseus knew of the Gorgons, but of how to find or kill them, he had no idea. Nevertheless he had given his promise, and though he saw now the satisfaction of King Polydectes, he was bound to keep his word. In his perplexity he prayed to the wise goddess, Athene, who came to him in a vision and promised him her aid.

"First, you must go," she said, "to the sisters Phorcides, who will tell you the way to the nymphs who guard the hat of darkness, the winged sandals, and the knapsack which can hold the Gorgon's head. Then I will give you a shield and my brother, Hermes, a sword which shall be made of adamant, the hardest rock. For nothing else can kill the Gorgon, since so venomous is her blood that a mortal sword when plunged in it is eaten away. But when you come to the Gorgons, invisible in your hat of darkness, turn your eyes away from them and look only on their reflection in your gleaming shield. Thus you may kill the monster without yourself being turned to stone. Pass her sisters by, for they are immortal, but smite off the head of Medusa with the hair of writhing snakes. Then put it in your knapsack and return, and I will be with you."

The vision ended, and with the aid of Athene, Perseus set out on the long journey to seek the Phorcides. These live in a dim cavern in the far north, where nights and days are one and where the whole earth is overspread with perpetual twilight. There sat the three old women mumbling to one another, crouched in a dim heap together, for they had but one eye and one tooth between them which they passed from hand to hand. Perseus came quietly behind them, and as they fumbled for the eye, he put his strong, brown hand next to one of the long, yellow ones, so that the old crone thought that it was her sister's and put the eye in it. There was a high scream of anger when they discovered the theft, and much clawing and groping in the dim recesses of the cavern. But they were helpless in their blindness and Perseus could laugh at them. At length for the price of their eye they told him how to reach the nymphs, and Perseus, laying the eye quickly in the hand of the nearest sister, fled as fast as he could before she could use it.

Again it was a far journey to the garden of the nymphs, where it is always sunshine and the trees bear golden apples. But the nymphs are friends of the wise gods and hate the monsters of darkness and the spirits of anger and despair. Therefore, they received Perseus with rejoicing and put the hat of darkness on his head, while on his feet they bound the golden, winged sandals, which are those Hermes wears when he runs down the slanting sunbeams or races along the

**4.** **◀ REREAD** Reread lines 53–68. What is heroic about the way Perseus responds to the request Polydectes makes? Support your answer with explicit textual evidence.

**5.** **READ ▶** As you read lines 82–154, continue to cite textual evidence.

- In the margin, explain why the Phorcides and the nymphs help Perseus.
- Underline details that create concern for Perseus.
- Circle the text that may be the climax—the exciting point in a story where a conflict is about to be resolved.

> "Their faces were neither snake nor woman, but part both . . ."

pathways of the wind. Next, Perseus put on his back the silver sack with the gleaming tassels of gold and flung across his shoulder the black-sheathed sword that was the gift of Hermes. On his left arm he fitted the shield that Athene gave, a gleaming silver shield like a mirror, plain without any marking. Then he sprang into the air and ran, invisible like the rushing wind, far out over the white-capped sea, across the yellow sands of the eastern desert, over strange streams and towering mountains, until at last he came to the shores of the distant ocean which flowed round all the world.

There was a grey gorge of stone by the ocean's edge, where lay Medusa and her sisters sleeping in the dim depths of the rock. All up and down the cleft the stones took fantastic shapes of trees, beasts, birds, or serpents. Here and there a man who had looked on the terrible Medusa stood forever with horror on his face. Far over the twilit gorge Perseus **hovered** invisible, while he loosened the pale, strange sword from its black sheath. Then with his face turned away and eyes on the silver shield he dropped, slow and silent as a falling leaf, down through the rocky cleft, twisting and turning past countless strange grey shapes, down from the bright sunlight into a chill, dim shadow echoing and re-echoing with the dashing of waves on the tumbled rocks beneath. There on the heaped stones lay the Gorgons sleeping together in the dimness, and even as he looked on them in the shield, Perseus felt stiff with horror at the sight.

hover:

Two of the Gorgons lay sprawled together, shaped like women yet scaled from head to foot as serpents are. Instead of hands they had gleaming claws like eagles, and their feet were dragons' feet. Skinny metallic wings like bats' wings hung from their shoulders. Their faces were neither snake nor woman, but part both, like faces in a nightmare. These two lay arm in arm and never stirred. Only the blue snakes still hissed and writhed round the pale, set face of Medusa, as

though even in sleep she were troubled by an evil dream. She lay by herself, arms outstretched, face upwards, more beautiful and terrible than living man may bear. All the crimes and madnesses of the world rushed into Perseus' mind as he gazed at her image in the shield. Horror stiffened his arm as he hovered over her with his sword uplifted. Then he shut his eyes to the vision and in the darkness struck.

There was a great cry and a hissing. Perseus groped for the head and seized it by the limp and snaky hair. Somehow he put it in his knapsack and was up and off, for at the dreadful scream the sister Gorgons had awakened. Now they were after him, their sharp claws grating against his silver shield. Perseus strained forward on the pathway of the wind like a runner, and behind him the two sisters came, smelling out the prey they could not see. Snakes darted from their girdles,[1] foam flew from their tusks, and the great wings beat the air. Yet the winged sandals were even swifter than they, and Perseus fled like the hunted deer with the speed of desperation. Presently the horrible noise grew faint behind him, the hissing of snakes and the sound of the bat wings died away. At last the Gorgons could smell him no longer and returned home unavenged.

[1] **girdles:** belts.

**6.** **REREAD** Reread lines 128–154. The resolution of a conflict may suggest a work's theme. What theme might be suggested by Perseus's triumph?

By now Perseus was over the Lybian desert, and as the blood from the horrible head touched the sand, it changed to serpents, from which the snakes of Africa are descended.

The storms of the Lybian desert blew against Perseus in clouds of eddying sand, until not even the divine sandals could hold him on his course. Far out to sea he was blown, and then north. Finally, whirled around the heavens like a cloud of mist, he alighted in the distant west where the giant, Atlas, held up on his shoulders the heavens from the earth. There the weary giant, crushed under the load of centuries, begged Perseus to show him Medusa's head. Perseus uncovered for him the dreadful thing, and Atlas was changed to the mighty mountain whose rocks rear up to reach the sky near the gateway to the Atlantic. Perseus himself, returning eastwards and still battling with the wind, was driven south to the land of Ethiopia, where king Cepheus reigned with his wife, Cassiopeia.

As Perseus came wheeling in like a gull from the ocean, he saw a strange sight. Far out to sea the water was troubled, seething and boiling as though stirred by a great force moving in its depths. Huge, sullen waves were starting far out and washing inland over sunken trees and flooded houses. Many miles of land were under water, and as he sped over them, he saw the muddy sea lapping around the foot of a black, upstanding rock. Here on a ledge above the water's edge stood a young girl chained by the arms, lips parted, eyes open and staring, face white as her linen garment. She might have been a statue, so still she stood, while the light breeze fluttered her dress and stirred her loosened hair. As Perseus looked at her and looked at the sea, the water began to boil again, and miles out a long, grey scaly back of vast length lifted itself above the flood. At that there was a shriek from a distant knoll where he could dimly see the forms of people, but the

**7.** **READ ▶** As you read lines 155–186, continue to cite text evidence.

- Circle the explanation of the origin of something found in nature.
- Underline what happens when Perseus shows Medusa's head to Atlas.
- Circle the author's description of the young girl in lines 170–186.

girl shrank a little and said nothing. Then Perseus, taking off the hat of darkness, alighted near the maiden to talk to her, and she, though nearly mad with terror, found words at last to tell him her tale.

Her name was Andromeda, and she was the only child of the king and of his wife, Cassiopeia. Queen Cassiopeia was exceedingly beautiful, so that all people marveled at her. She herself was proud of her dark eyes, her white, slender fingers, and her long black hair, so proud that she had been heard to boast that she was fairer even than the sea nymphs who are daughters of Nereus. At this Nereus in **wrath** stirred up Poseidon,[2] who came flooding in over the land, covering it far and wide. Not content with this he sent a vast monster from the dark depths of the bottomless sea to ravage the whole coast of Ethiopia. When the unfortunate king and queen had sought the advice of the oracle on how to appease the god, they had been ordered to sacrifice their only daughter to the sea monster Poseidon had sent. Not daring for their people's sake to disobey, they had chained her to this rock, where she now awaited the beast who should devour her.

**wrath:**

Perseus comforted Andromeda as he stood by her on the rock, and she shrank closer against him while the great, grey back writhed its half-mile length slowly towards the land. Then bidding Andromeda hide her face, Perseus sprang once more into the air,

[2] **Poseidon:** in Greek mythology, the god of the seas.

**8.** **◀ REREAD** Reread lines 158–169. Why does Atlas beg Perseus to show him Medusa's head? Cite explicit textual evidence in your response.

**9.** **READ ▶** As you read lines 187–212, continue to cite text evidence.

- Circle what Queen Cassiopeia does to make Nereus so angry.
- In the margin, summarize what has happened to Andromeda in lines 187–200.
- Underline what happens when Perseus shows Medusa's head to the sea monster.

unveiling the dreadful head of dead Medusa to the monster which reared its dripping jaws yards high into the air. The mighty tail stiffened all of a sudden, the boiling of the water ceased, and only the gentle waves of the receding ocean lapped around a long, grey ridge of stone. Then Perseus freed Andromeda and restored her to her father and beautiful mother. Thereafter with their consent he married her amid scenes of tremendous rejoicing, and with his bride set sail at last for the kingdom of Polydectes.

Polydectes had lost no time on the departure of Perseus. First he had begged Danae to become his wife, and then he had threatened her. Undoubtedly he would have got his way by force if Danae had not fled in terror to Dictys. The two took refuge at the altar of a temple whence Polydectes did not dare drag them away. So matters stood when Perseus returned. Polydectes was enraged to see him, for he had hoped at least that Danae's most powerful protector would never return. But now, seeing him famous and with a king's daughter to wife, he could not contain himself. Openly he laughed at the tale of Perseus, saying that the hero had never killed the Gorgon, only pretended to, and that now he was claiming an honor he did not

**10.** **REREAD** Reread lines 201–212. What is heroic about Perseus's rescue of Andromeda?

**11.** **READ** As you read lines 213–252, continue to cite textual evidence.

- Circle the resolution of the conflict between Perseus and Polydectes.
- Underline Perseus's action in lines 228–235 that shows his gratitude to the gods.
- In the margin, explain how the earlier prophecy of Apollo is fulfilled in lines 242–252.

> "You asked me for the Gorgon's head. Behold it!"

deserve. At this Perseus, enraged by the insult and by reports of his mother's persecution, said to him, "You asked me for the Gorgon's head. Behold it!" And with that he lifted it high, and Polydectes became stone.

Then Perseus left Dictys to be king of that island, but he himself went back to the Grecian mainland to seek out his grandfather, Acrisios, who was once again king of Argos. First, however, he gave back to the gods the gifts they had given him. Hermes took back the golden sandals and the hat of darkness, for both are his. But Athene took Medusa's head, and she hung it on a fleece around her neck as part of her battle equipment, where it may be seen in statues and portraits of the warlike goddess.

Perseus took ship for Greece, but his fame had gone before him, and king Acrisios fled secretly from Argos in terror, since he remembered the prophecy and feared that Perseus had come to avenge the wrongs of Danae. The trembling old Acrisios took refuge in Larissa, where it happened the king was holding a great athletic contest in honor of his dead father.

Heroes from all over Greece, among whom was Perseus, came to the games. As Perseus was competing at the discus throwing, he threw high into the air and far beyond the rest. A strong wind caught the discus as it spun so that it left the course marked out for it and was carried into the stands. People scrambled away to right and left.

Only Acrisios was not nimble enough. The heavy weight fell full on his foot and crushed his toes, and at that the feeble old man, already weakened by his terrors, died from the shock. Thus the prophecy of Apollo was fulfilled at last; Acrisios was killed by his grandson. Then Perseus came into his kingdom, where he reigned with Andromeda long and happily.

**12.** **REREAD AND DISCUSS** Reread lines 228–252. In a small group, discuss what is ironic, or unexpected, about Acrisios's death. Cite explicit textual evidence in your discussion.

## SHORT RESPONSE

*Cite Text Evidence* What theme, or central idea about life, is expressed in this myth? Consider the way conflicts are resolved and the way characters behave. Review your reading notes and **cite text evidence** in your response.

1. READ ▶ As you read lines 1–36 of the poem, collect and cite text evidence.
   - Circle the questions Medusa asks.
   - In lines 15–27, underline what Medusa threatens to do. In the margin, make an inference about her character.
   - In the margin, summarize what happens in the last stanza.

## Medusa

Poem by Agha Shahid Ali

"I must be beautiful.
Or why would men be speechless
at my sight? I have populated the countryside
with animals of stone
and put nations painlessly to sleep.
I too was human, I who now live here
at the end of the world
with two aging sisters, spinsters
massaging poisons into our scalps
and sunning our ruffled snakes,

and dreading the night, when
under the warm stars
we recall men we have loved,
their gestures now forever refusing us.

Then why let anything remain
when whatever we loved
turned instantly to stone?
I am waiting for the Mediterranean
to see me: It will petrify.
And as caravans from Africa begin to cross it,
I will freeze their cargo of slaves.

Soon, soon, the sky will have eyes:
I will fossilize its dome into cracked blue,
I who am about to come
into God's full view
from the wrong side of the mirror
into which He gazes."

And so she dreams
till the sun-crimsoned shield
blinds her into nightmare;
her locks, failing from their roots,
crawl into rocks to die.
Perseus holds the sword above her neck.
Restless in her sleep, she,
for the last time, brushes back
the hissing curls from her forehead.

2. **REREAD AND DISCUSS** With a small group, discuss the way Medusa is presented in the poem. In what way does learning her thoughts and feelings affect your view of her? Cite text evidence in your discussion.

## SHORT RESPONSE

*Cite Text Evidence* How do "Medusa's Head" and "Medusa" differ in their presentation of Medusa? Review your reading notes, and be sure to **cite evidence from the text** in your response.

**Background** **Mark Twain** *(1835–1910) is probably America's most celebrated humorist. Born Samuel L. Clemens in Hannibal, Missouri, Twain wrote a number of classic novels including* The Prince and the Pauper. *You are about to read three versions of a scene from* The Prince and the Pauper: *an excerpt from Twain's novel, a dramatization by* **Joellen Brand,** *and a graphic story by* **Marvel Comics.** *In the scene that follows, a poor boy named Tom Canty hopes to catch a glimpse of Edward Tudor, the Prince of Wales.*

## COMPARING VERSIONS OF

# The Prince and the Pauper

**CLOSE READ** Notes

1. **READ ▶** As you read lines 1–45, begin to collect text evidence.
   - In the margin, explain what "the desire of Tom's soul" is (line 5).
   - Underline details that describe the boy who Tom sees.
   - Circle phrases that show the prince's kindness to Tom.

## Tom's Meeting with the Prince.

*from* the Novel by Mark Twain

Tom got up hungry, and sauntered hungry away, but with his thoughts busy with the shadowy splendours of his night's dreams. He idled down a quiet, lovely road, past the great cardinal's stately palace, toward a far more mighty and **majestic** palace beyond—Westminster. Was the desire of his soul to be satisfied at last? Here, indeed, was a king's palace. Might he not hope to see a prince now—a prince of flesh and blood, if Heaven were willing?

**majestic:**

Poor little Tom, in his rags, approached, and was moving slowly and timidly past the sentinels, with a beating heart and a rising hope, when all at once he caught sight through the golden bars of a spectacle that almost made him shout for joy. Within was a comely boy, tanned and brown with sturdy outdoor sports and exercises, whose clothing was all of lovely silks and satins, shining with jewels; at his hip a little jewelled sword and dagger; dainty buskins[1] on his feet, with red heels;

[1] **buskin:** thick-soled laced boot that reaches to the calf.

and on his head a jaunty crimson cap, with drooping plumes fastened with a great sparkling gem. Several gorgeous gentlemen stood near—his servants, without a doubt. Oh! He was a prince—a prince, a living prince, a real prince—without the shadow of a question; and the prayer of the pauper-boy's heart was answered at last.

Tom's breath came quick and short with excitement, and his eyes grew big with wonder and delight. Everything gave way in his mind instantly to one desire: that was to get close to the prince, and have a good, devouring look at him. Before he knew what he was about, he had his face against the gate-bars. The next instant one of the soldiers snatched him rudely away, and sent him spinning among the gaping crowd of country gawks and London idlers. The soldier said,—

"Mind thy manners, thou young beggar!"

The crowd jeered and laughed; but the young prince sprang to the gate with his face flushed, and his eyes flashing with indignation, and cried out,—

"How dar'st thou use a poor lad like that? How dar'st thou use the King my father's meanest subject so? Open the gates, and let him in!"

You should have seen that fickle crowd snatch off their hats then. You should have heard them cheer, and shout, "Long live the Prince of Wales!"

The soldiers presented arms with their halberds,[2] opened the gates, and presented again as the little Prince of Poverty passed in, in his fluttering rags, to join hands with the Prince of Limitless Plenty.

[2] **halberd:** a weapon that resembles a battle-ax.

**2.** REREAD Reread lines 27–41. What does the prince's treatment of Tom reveal about his character? Cite text evidence in your response.

______________________________

______________________________

**3.** READ As you read lines 46–111, continue to cite text evidence.

- Underline the questions the prince asks Tom.
- In the margin, describe the prince's reaction to what Tom says in lines 57–64.
- Circle the prince's reactions to Tom's description of home in lines 79–111. In the margin, paraphrase what the prince says in lines 102–105.

Edward Tudor said—

"Thou lookest tired and hungry: thou'st been treated ill. Come with me."

Edward took Tom to a rich apartment in the palace, which he called his cabinet. By his command a repast was brought such as Tom had never encountered before except in books. The prince sat near by, and asked questions while Tom ate.

"What is thy name, lad?"

"Tom Canty, an' it please thee, sir."

"'Tis an odd one. Where dost live?"

"In the city, please thee, sir. Offal[3] Court, out of Pudding Lane."

"Offal Court! Truly 'tis another odd one. Hast parents?"

"Parents have I, sir, and a grand-dam likewise that is but indifferently precious to me, God forgive me if it be offence to say it—also twin sisters, Nan and Bet."

"Then is thy grand-dam not over kind to thee, I take it?"

"Neither to any other is she, so please your worship."

"Doth she mistreat thee?"

"There be times that she stayeth her hand, being asleep or overcome with drink; but when she hath her judgment clear again, she maketh it up to me with goodly beatings."

A fierce look came into the little prince's eyes, and he cried out—

"What! Beatings?"

"Oh, indeed, yes, please you, sir."

"*Beatings*!—and thou so frail and little. Is thy father kind to thee?"

"Not more than Gammer Canty, sir."

"Fathers be alike, mayhap. Mine hath not a doll's temper. He smiteth with a heavy hand, yet spareth me: he spareth me not always with his tongue, though, sooth to say. How doth thy mother use thee?"

"She is good, sir, and giveth me neither sorrow nor pain of any sort. And Nan and Bet are like to her in this."

"How old be these?"

"Fifteen, an' it please you, sir."

"Thou speakest well; thou hast an easy grace in it. Art learned?"

"I know not if I am or not, sir. The good priest that is called Father Andrew taught me, of his kindness, from his books."

"Know'st thou the Latin?"

---

[3] **Offal:** waste or garbage.

"But scantly, sir, I doubt."

"Tell me of thy Offal Court. Hast thou a pleasant life there?"

"In truth, yes, so please you, sir, save when one is hungry. There be Punch-and-Judy[4] shows, and monkeys—oh such antic creatures! and so bravely dressed!—and there be plays wherein they that play do shout and fight till all are slain, and 'tis so fine to see, and costeth but a farthing[5]—albeit 'tis main hard to get the farthing, please your worship."

"Tell me more."

"We lads of Offal Court do strive against each other with the cudgel, like to the fashion of the 'prentices, sometimes."

The prince's eyes flashed. Said he—

"Marry, that would not I mislike. Tell me more."

"We strive in races, sir, to see who of us shall be fleetest."

"That would I like also. Speak on."

"In summer, sir, we wade and swim in the canals and in the river, and each doth duck his neighbour, and splatter him with water, and dive and shout and tumble and—"

"'Twould be worth my father's kingdom but to enjoy it once! Prithee go on."

"We dance and sing about the Maypole in Cheapside; we play in the sand, each covering his neighbour up; and times we make mud pastry—oh the lovely mud, it hath not its like for delightfulness in all the world!—we do fairly wallow in the mud, sir, saving your worship's presence."

[4] **Punch-and-Judy show:** traditional puppet show. The puppets are Mr. Punch and his wife Judy, who get into comical fights.

[5] **farthing:** a former British coin worth one-fourth of a penny.

4. **REREAD AND DISCUSS** Reread lines 78–111. In a small group, discuss which elements of Tom's life most appeal to the prince. Cite text evidence in your discussion.

5. **READ** As you read lines 112–156, continue to cite textual evidence.
   - Underline what the boys realize after they switch clothes.
   - Circle what the prince sees on Tom's hand. In the margin, explain the Prince's reaction.
   - In the margin, explain what happens in lines 139–156.

"Oh, prithee, say no more, 'tis glorious! If that I could but clothe me in raiment like to thine, and strip my feet, and revel in the mud once, just once, with none to rebuke me or forbid, meseemeth I could forego the crown!"

"And if that I could clothe me once, sweet sir, as thou art clad—just once—"

"Oho, would'st like it? Then so shall it be. Doff thy rags, and don these splendours, lad! It is a brief happiness, but will be not less keen for that. We will have it while we may, and change again before any come to molest."

A few minutes later the little Prince of Wales was garlanded with Tom's fluttering odds and ends, and the little Prince of Pauperdom was tricked out in the **gaudy** plumage of royalty. The two went and stood side by side before a great mirror, and lo, a miracle: there did not seem to have been any change made! They stared at each other, then at the glass, then at each other again. At last the puzzled princeling said—

**gaudy:**

"What dost thou make of this?"

"Ah, good your worship, require me not to answer. It is not meet that one of my degree should utter the thing."

"Then will *I* utter it. Thou hast the same hair, the same eyes, the same voice and manner, the same form and stature, the same face and countenance that I bear. Fared we forth naked, there is none could say which was you, and which the Prince of Wales. And, now that I am clothed as thou wert clothed, it seemeth I should be able the more nearly to feel as thou didst when the brute soldier—Hark ye, is not this a bruise upon your hand?"

"Yes; but it is a slight thing, and your worship knoweth that the poor man-at-arms—"

"Peace! It was a shameful thing and a cruel!" cried the little prince, stamping his bare foot. "If the King—Stir not a step till I come again! It is a command!"

In a moment he had snatched up and put away an article of national importance that lay upon a table, and was out at the door and flying through the palace grounds in his bannered rags, with a hot face and glowing eyes. As soon as he reached the great gate, he seized the bars, and tried to shake them, shouting—

"Open! Unbar the gates!"

The soldier that had maltreated Tom obeyed promptly; and as the prince burst through the portal, half-smothered with royal wrath, the soldier fetched him a sounding box on the ear that sent him whirling to the roadway, and said—

"Take that, thou beggar's spawn, for what thou got'st me from his Highness!"

The crowd roared with laughter. The prince picked himself out of the mud, and made fiercely at the sentry, shouting—

"I am the Prince of Wales, my person is sacred; and thou shalt hang for laying thy hand upon me!"

The soldier brought his halberd to a present-arms and said **mockingly**—

mockingly:

"I salute your gracious Highness." Then angrily—"Be off, thou crazy rubbish!"

Here the jeering crowd closed round the poor little prince, and hustled him far down the road, hooting him, and shouting—

"Way for his Royal Highness! Way for the Prince of Wales!"

**6.** REREAD Reread lines 122–156. How does Tom and the prince's discovery help you understand what happens after the prince leaves Tom? Support your answer with explicit textual evidence.

## SHORT RESPONSE

*Cite Text Evidence* Why might the prince want to trade places with Tom? Think about what you know of the prince's character. Review your reading notes and be sure to **cite text evidence** in your response.

**CLOSE READ** Notes

1. **READ ▶** As you read the introductory text and lines 1–25, begin to collect and cite text evidence.
   - Underline details in the setting that suggest royalty.
   - Underline stage directions that describe Tom's appearance and behavior.
   - Circle the prince's dialogue. In the margin, explain what his response to events tells you about him.

## *from* The Prince and the Pauper

Dramatization by Joellen Bland

**CHARACTERS**

**Edward,** Prince of Wales
**Tom Canty,** the Pauper
**Two Women**
**Two Guards**
**Villagers**

**Time:** *1547.*

**Setting:** *Westminster Palace, England. Gates leading to courtyard are at right. Slightly to the left, off courtyard and inside gates,* ***interior*** *of palace anteroom[1] is visible. There is a couch with a rich robe draped on it, screen at rear, bellcord, mirror, chairs, and a table with bowl of nuts, and a large golden seal on it. Piece of armor hangs on one wall. Exits are rear and downstage.*

**interior:**

### Scene One

**At Curtain Rise.** Two Guards—*one at right, one at left—stand in front of gates, several* Villagers *hover nearby, straining to see into courtyard where* Prince *may be seen through fence, playing.* Two Women *enter right.*

**1st Woman.** I have walked all morning just to have a glimpse of Westminster Palace.

**2nd Woman.** Maybe if we can get near enough to the gates, we can have a glimpse of the young Prince. (Tom Canty, *dirty and ragged, comes out of crowd and steps close to gates.*)

**Tom.** I have always dreamed of seeing a real prince! (*Excited, he presses his nose against gates.*)

[1] **anteroom:** an outer room that leads to an inner room and is often used as a waiting room.

**1st Guard.** Mind your manners, you young beggar! (*Seizes* Tom *by collar and sends him sprawling into crowd.* Villagers *laugh, as* Tom *slowly gets to his feet.*)

**Prince** (*rushing to gates*). How dare you treat a poor subject of the King in such a manner! Open the gates and let him in! (*As* Villagers *see* Prince, *they take off their hats and bow low.*)

**Villagers** (*shouting together*). Long live the Prince of Wales! (Guards *open gates and* Tom *slowly passes through, as if in a dream.*)

**Prince** (*to* Tom). You look tired, and you have been treated cruelly. I am Edward, Prince of Wales. What is your name?

**Tom** (*looking around in awe*). Tom Canty, Your Highness.

**Prince.** Come into the palace with me, Tom. (Prince *leads* Tom *into anteroom.* Villagers *pantomime conversation, and all but a few exit.*) Where do you live, Tom?

**Tom.** In the city, Your Highness, in Offal Court.

**Prince.** Offal Court? That's an odd name. Do you have parents?

**Tom.** Yes, Your Highness.

**Prince.** How does your father treat you?

**Tom.** If it please you, Your Highness, when I am not able to beg a penny for our supper, he treats me to beatings.

**Prince** (*shocked*). What! Beatings? My father is not a calm man, but he does not beat me. (*looks at* Tom *thoughtfully*) You speak well and have an easy grace. Have you been schooled?

**Tom.** Very little, Your Highness. A good priest who shares our house in Offal Court has taught me from his books.

**2.** ◀ **REREAD** Reread lines 8–22. In what ways do the stage directions help you understand Tom's character? Cite text evidence in your response.

______________________________________________

______________________________________________

**3.** **READ** ▶ As you read lines 26–48, continue to cite textual evidence.

- Underline what Tom tells the prince about life at Offal Court.
- Circle the stage direction that describes the prince's reaction when he learns that Tom's father hits him.
- In the margin, explain what each character wants.

**Prince.** Do you have a pleasant life in Offal Court?

**Tom.** Pleasant enough, Your Highness, save when I am hungry. We have Punch and Judy shows, and sometimes we lads have fights in the street.

**Prince** (*eagerly*). I should like that. Tell me more.

**Tom.** In summer, we run races and swim in the river, and we love to wallow in the mud.

**Prince** (*sighing,* ***wistfully***). If I could wear your clothes and play in the mud just once, with no one to forbid me, I think I could give up the crown!

**wistfully:**

**Tom** (*shaking his head*). And if I could wear your fine clothes just once, Your Highness . . .

**Prince.** Would you like that? Come, then. We shall change places. You can take off your rags and put on my clothes—and I will put on yours. (*He leads* Tom *behind screen, and they return shortly, each wearing the other's clothes.*) Let's look at ourselves in this mirror. (*leads* Tom *to mirror*)

**Tom.** Oh, Your Highness, it is not proper for me to wear such clothes.

**Prince** (*excitedly, as he looks in the mirror*). Heavens, do you not see it? We look like brothers! We have the same features and bearing.[2] If we went about together, dressed alike, there is no one who could say which is the Prince of Wales and which is Tom Canty!

**Tom** (*drawing back and rubbing his hand*). Your Highness, I am frightened. . . .

**Prince.** Do not worry. (*seeing* Tom *rub his hand*) Is that a bruise on your hand?

**Tom.** Yes, but it is slight thing, Your Highness.

**Prince** (*angrily*). It was shameful and cruel of that guard to strike you. Do not stir a step until I come back. I command you! (*He picks up the golden Seal of England*[3] *and carefully puts it into a piece of armor. He then dashes out to gates.*) Open! Unbar the gates at once! (2nd Guard

---

[2] **features and bearing:** parts of the face and ways of standing and walking.

[3] **Seal of England:** a device used to stamp a special design, usually a picture of the ruler, onto a document, thus indicating that it has royal approval.

**4. READ ▷** As you read lines 49–79, continue to cite textual evidence.

- In the margin, explain why Tom is "frightened" (line 60).
- Circle how the guards and villagers treat the prince when he leaves the palace in Tom's clothes.

*opens gates, and as* Prince *runs out, in rags,* 1st Guard *seizes him, boxes him on the ear, and knocks him to the ground.)*

**1st Guard.** Take that, you little beggar, for the trouble you have made for me with the Prince. (Villagers *roar with laughter.*)

**Prince** (*picking himself up, turning on* Guard *furiously*). I am Prince of Wales! You shall hang for laying your hand on me!

**1st Guard** (*presenting arms; mockingly*). I salute Your Gracious Highness! (*then, angrily,* 1st Guard *shoves* Prince *roughly aside.*) Be off, you mad bag of rags! (Prince *is surrounded by* Villagers, *who hustle him off.*)

**Villagers** (*ad lib, as they exit, shouting*). Make way for His Royal Highness! Make way for the Prince of Wales! Hail to the Prince! (*Etc.*)

**5.** **◀ REREAD AND DISCUSS** Reread lines 1–79. In a small group, discuss how the plot unfolds to create a conflict at the end of this scene. Cite explicit textual evidence in your discussion.

## SHORT RESPONSE

*Cite Text Evidence* How do the stage directions and the dialogue help you understand the characters of Tom and the prince? Be sure to **cite text evidence** in your response.

1. **READ ▶** As you read the first two pages of the graphic story, begin to collect and cite textual evidence.
   - Underline Tom's feelings about the palace and the prince.
   - Circle text that shows the prince's character.

## *from* The Prince and the Pauper

Graphic Story by Marvel Comics

PRINCE EDWARD TOOK TOM TO A RICH APARTMENT IN THE PALACE, WHICH HE CALLED HIS CABINET.
BY EDWARD'S COMMAND A REPAST WAS BROUGHT SUCH AS TOM HAD NEVER ENCOUNTERED BEFORE... EXCEPT IN BOOKS.
WHAT IS THY NAME, LAD?
TOM CANTY, AN' IT PLEASE THEE, SIR.
HAST THEE PARENTS?
PARENTS HAVE I, SIR, AND A GRANDAM LIKEWISE... ALSO TWIN SISTERS, NAN AND BET.
MY GRANDAM HAS A WICKED HEART AND WORKETH EVIL ALL OF HER DAYS. SHE GIVES ME GOODLY BEATINGS.
BEATINGS!
AND THOU SO FRAIL AND LITTLE. TELL ME MORE OF THIS PLACE YOU LIVE.
IF ONE SURVIVES THE BEATINGS AND HUNGER, SIR, WE WADE AND SWIM IN THE CANALS, AND EACH DOTH DUCK HIS NEIGHBOR, AND DIVE AND SHOUT--
'TWOULD BE WORTH MY FATHER'S KINGDOM BUT TO ENJOY SUCH ONCE. IF I COULD REVEL IN THE MUD JUST ONCE, WITH NONE TO REBUKE ME!
AND IF I COULD CLOTHE ME ONCE, SWEET SIR, AS THOU ART CLAD...
OHO! WOULDST LIKE IT? THEN SO SHALL IT BE! DOFF THY RAGS AND DON THESE SPLENDORS, LAD!
IT IS A BRIEF HAPPINESS, BUT WILL BE NOT LESS KEEN FOR THAT.
WHAT DOST THOU MAKE OF THIS?
AH, GOOD YOUR WORSHIP REQUIRE ME NOT TO ANSWER.
THEN I WILL UTTER IT. FARED WE BOTH NAKED THERE IS NONE COULD SAY WHICH WAS YOU--
--AND WHICH THE PRINCE OF WALES!

**2.** **REREAD** Reread the page above. How do the illustrations convey that the boys look alike? Circle illustrations that help you recognize their similarities.

3. **READ ▶** As you read this page, continue to cite textual evidence.

- Circle the dialogue that is shown with jagged outlines. In the margin, explain why the artist has used these outlines.
- In the margin, paraphrase what the guard says to the prince.
- Circle the prince's facial expression in the last panel.

4. REREAD AND DISCUSS The only time we see the prince's reaction to being thrown out is in the graphic story. In a small group, discuss how learning the prince's reaction impacts your perception of events.

## SHORT RESPONSE

*Cite Text Evidence* Analyze the way you learn about Tom and the prince's similarities in the three versions of the story. Which version was most effective? Review your reading notes and **cite text evidence** in your response.

# Acknowledgments

Excerpt from *The Bat Scientists* (Retitled: "Bats!") by Mary Kay Carson. Text copyright © 2010 by Mary Kay Carson. Reprinted by permission of Houghton Mifflin Harcourt Publishing Company.

"Community Hero: Chief Wilma Mankiller" by Susannah Abbey from www.myhero.com. Text copyright © 2010 by The My Hero Project, Inc. Reprinted by permission of The My Hero Project, Inc.

Excerpt from *The Discovery of the Titanic* by Dr. Robert D. Ballard with Rich Archbold. Text copyright © 1987, 1989 by Ballard & Family. Reprinted by permission of Madison Press Books.

Excerpt from *Every Day Is a Good Day: Reflections by Contemporary Indigenous Women* (Retitled: "from Every Day is a New Day") by Wilma Mankiller. Text copyright © 2004, 2011 by Wilma Mankiller. Reprinted by permission of Fulcrum Publishing.

"Face Your Fears" (Retitled: "Face Your Fears: Choking Under Pressure Is Every Athlete's Worst Nightmare") by Dana Hudepohl from *Sports Illustrated for Women,* February 12, 2001. Text copyright © 2001 by CNN/Sports Illustrated. Reprinted by permission of CNN/Sports Illustrated.

"Face Your Fears and Scare the Phobia Out of Your Brain" by Jason Koebler from www.usnews.com, May 21, 2012. Text copyright © 2012 by U.S. News & World Report LP. Reprinted by permission of U.S. News & World Report LP.

Excerpt from *The Jumping Tree* by René Saldaña, Jr. Text copyright © 2001 by René Saldaña, Jr. Reprinted by permission of Random House, Inc.

"The Light—Ah! The Light" from *Eureka! Poems About Inventors* by Joyce Sidman. Text copyright © 2002 by Joyce Sidman. Reprinted by permission of Lerner Publishing Group.

"Medusa" from *A Nostalgist's Map of America: Poems* by Agha Shahid Ali. Text copyright © 1992 by Agha Shahid Ali. Reprinted by permission of W.W. Norton & Company.

"Medusa's Head" from *Greek Myths* by Olivia E. Coolidge. Text copyright © 1949, renewed 1977 by Olivia E. Coolidge. Reprinted by permission of Houghton Mifflin Harcourt Publishing Company.

"*Moby-Duck* Book Review" by David Holahan, from www.csmonitor.com, April 5, 2011. Text copyright © 2011 by David Holahan. Reprinted by permission of David Holahan.

"On the Titanic, Defined by What They Wore" by Guy Trebay from *The New York Times,* April 11, 2012, www.nytimes.com. Text copyright © 2012 by The New York Times Company. Reprinted by permission of PARS International on behalf of The New York Times.

"The Pod" by Maureen Crane Wartski from *Boy's Life* Magazine, August 2012. Text copyright © 2012 by Maureen Crane Wartski. Published by the Boy Scouts of America. Reprinted by permission of Maureen Crane Wartski.

"The Prince and the Pauper" by Mark Twain, adapted by Joellen Bland from *Stage Plays from the Classics.* Text copyright © 1987, 2000, 2005 by PLAYS, The Drama Magazine for Young People/Sterling Partners, Inc. Reprinted by permission of Kalmbach Publishing Company.

Excerpt from *Stan Lee Presents The Prince and the Pauper by Mark Twain.* Copyright © 1978 by Marvel Characters, Inc. Reprinted by permission of Marvel Entertainment.

"There Will Come Soft Rains" by Ray Bradbury. Text copyright © 1950 by the Crowell-Collier Publishing Company, renewed 1977 by Ray Bradbury. Reprinted by permission of Don Congdon Associates, Inc.

"What Do Fish Have to Do with Anything?" from *What Do Fish Have to Do With Anything?* by Avi. Text Copyright © 1997 by Avi. Reprinted by permission of Candlewick Press, Somerville, MA and Brandt & Hochman Literary Agents, Inc.

# Index of Titles & Authors


**A**

Abbey, Susannah, 87
Ali, Agha Shahid, 101, 113
*Association of Zoos and Aquariums*, 66
Avi, 69

**B**

*Bats!*, 29
Bland, Joellen, 115, 121
Bradbury, Ray, 43

**C**

*Can Animals Feel and Think?*, 25
Carson, Mary Kay, 29
*Community Hero: Chief Wilma Mankiller*, 87
Coolidge, Olivia E., 101

**E**

*Every Day Is a New Day*, from, 87, 91

**F**

*Face Your Fears and Scare the Phobias Out of Your Brain*, 13
*Face Your Fears: Choking Under Pressure Is Every Athlete's Worst Nightmare*, 9
*Functions of a Zoo*, 63

**H**

Holahan, David, 37
Hudepohl, Dana, 9

**I**

*Innocent and Imprisoned*, 67

**J**

Jones, DeShawn, 25
*Jumping Tree*, from *The*, 3

**K**

Koebler, Jason, 13

**L**

*Light—Ah! The Light, The*, 97

**M**

McGuinness, Robert, 67
Mankiller, Wilma, 87, 91
Marvel Comics, 115, 125
*Medusa* 101, 113
*Medusa's Head*, 101
*Moby-Duck*, 37

**O**

*On the Titanic, Defined by What They Wore*, 53

**P**

*Pod, The*, 19
*Prince and the Pauper* (Drama), from *The*, 115, 121
*Prince and the Pauper* (Graphic Story), from *The*, 115, 125
*Prince and the Pauper* (Novel): *Tom's Meeting with the Prince*, from *The*, 115

**S**

Saldaña Jr., René, 3
Sidman, Joyce, 97
*Sonia's Blog: Who I Am, What I Do—Every Day*, 64

**T**

*There Will Come Soft Rains*, 43
Trebay, Guy, 53
Twain, Mark, 115

**V**

*Views on Zoos*, 63

**W**

Wartski, Maureen Crane, 19
*What Do Fish Have to Do with Anything?*, 69